7

£1.50
11/∠

F/I

MARGERY FISH'S
Country Gardening

Timothy Clark

DAVID & CHARLES
Newton Abbot · London

ACKNOWLEDGEMENTS

My thanks to Henry Boyd-Carpenter for advice and free access to all of Margery Fish's written works; to Tony Venison and *Country Life* for recognising the loss to our gardening heritage if the garden at East Lambrook had been allowed to perish; to Valerie Finnis for colour photographs; to Derek Tilley, a previous editor of *The Field* for the black and white photographs; to Andrew Norton for the lists of plants; to the gardening acquaintances of Margery Fish for their anecdotes and memories and to Barbara Rooney for typing.

PAGE 2
Against the cowhouse, *Stauntonia, Rosa* Caroline Testout and
Euphorbia wulfenii were planted for the summer

British Library Cataloguing in Publication Data

Clark, Timothy
    Margery Fish's country gardening.
    1. Great Britain. Country gardens.
    Design
    I. Title
    712'.6'0941

ISBN 0-7153-9059-7

Text © Timothy Clark 1989
Colour photographs © Valerie Finnis 1989

Typeset in 11/14pt Plantin Light
by Typesetters (Birmingham) Ltd,
Smethwick, West Midlands
Colour origination by Columbia Offset (UK) Ltd
Printed in Great Britain
by Butler & Tanner Limited, Frome and London
for David & Charles Publishers plc
Brunel House Newton Abbot Devon

Contents

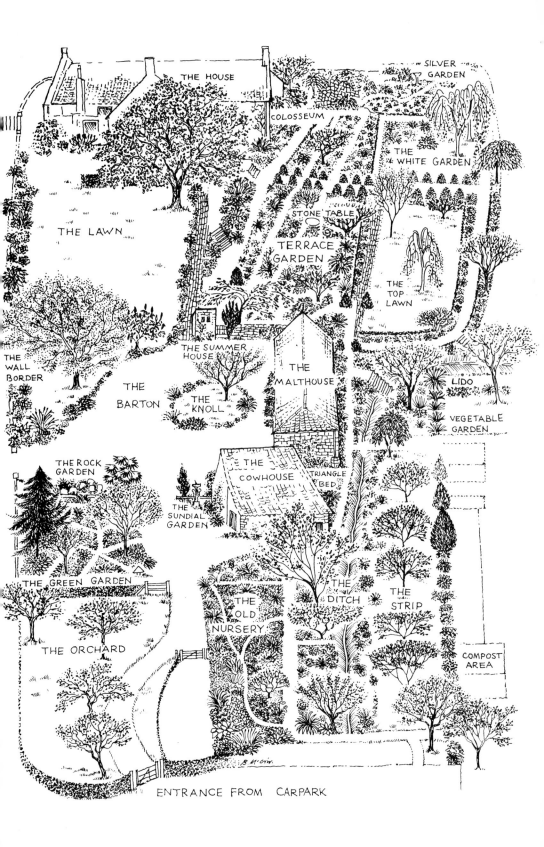

THE HOUSE

SILVER GARDEN

COLOSSEUM

THE WHITE GARDEN

STONE TABLE

TERRACE GARDEN

THE LAWN

THE TOP LAWN

THE WALL BORDER

THE SUMMER HOUSE

THE MALTHOUSE

LIDO

THE BARTON

THE KNOLL

VEGETABLE GARDEN

THE ROCK GARDEN

THE COWHOUSE

TRIANGLE BED

THE SUNDIAL GARDEN

THE GREEN GARDEN

THE OLD NURSERY

THE DITCH

THE STRIP

THE ORCHARD

COMPOST AREA

ENTRANCE FROM CARPARK

1

Introduction

Margery Fish is one of the most important gardeners to have emerged in the British Isles since the Second World War. Her garden and her books instructed and inspired hundreds of gardeners. Her interest in the genuine cottage garden was far removed from the *cottage orné* style of the Edwardians. Her work in re-discovering and distributing the old florists' flowers as well as the rarer forms of local wild flowers is recognised for its pioneering spirit by the present generation of gardeners; the cultivars she developed are widely grown in our gardens; her *Gardening in the Shade* was a particularly original book.

Born Margery Townsend at Stanford Hill in London in 1892 and educated at the Friends' School at Saffron Walden, Essex, she entered Fleet Street as Lord Northcliffe's secretary. She remained at the *Daily Mail* as secretary to each successive editor, until she married Walter Fish, and in 1937 left London.

They purchased East Lambrook Manor at South Petherton, near Ilminster, Somerset, for £1000, and immediately commenced restoring and creating the small but internationally famous garden that exists today. For some time she relied heavily upon Walter's advice, and followed his decisions. As the years progressed so she grew in confidence, and in 1949 when he died she emerged in her own right. By 1953 she was a well-known popular gardening writer and lecturer who travelled the British Isles with missionary zeal. She disseminated her knowledge in three ways – by lecturing, by her books, and with the nursery she established to make her plants available to an increasingly knowledgeable public.

Her style of gardening was dominated by the terrain of her garden; its small areas of sun, shade, marsh, stream and orchard did not lend themselves to the massed herbaceous borders and grand style of previous generations. Nor did she hanker for the formal gradation of colour which Gertrude Jekyll had popularised for fifty years. Her primary

objective was the creation of a garden which every day of the year had its seasonal complement of flowers; it was to be a typical English cottage garden, in keeping with the small manor-house, and with the plants as the main feature, maintenance must be simple. She achieved a garden that Francis Boyd-Carpenter, her brother-in-law, estimated had usually over 2,000 cultivars, but never gave the appearance of a nursery nor had too many varieties of doubtful hardiness or too similar to the species.

The plants she grew were mainly of two groups – the general herbaceous plants, from Artemesia Lambrook Silver for the silver garden, to hellebores, senecios and sedums, plants that would provide colour through the year; and her first love, the plants of the English cottage garden. For these her search was tireless. In a period when old buildings were being pulled down at an alarming rate, she realised the memories of these old gardens would soon be all that was left. She made a home for plants that were not sufficiently fashionable to survive the changing face of English gardening during the 1950s and 60s. No definite design or attention to saving labour ever attended a cottage garden, though the close jostling friendliness she obtained by placing disparate plants together did largely smother weeds.

As her gardening knowledge expanded she commenced writing, with articles in *Amateur Gardening* and *The Field*. Her first book *We Made a Garden* was published in 1956. Her writing style was enthusiastic and infectiously readable. She immediately created for herself a following of gardeners who learnt from her readily admitted mistakes and had their eyes opened to a wider range of plants and how to use them. By the time she finished writing she had produced eight books dealing with every aspect of her garden experience: *We Made a Garden* (1956), *An All the Year Garden* (1958), *Cottage Garden Flowers* (1961), *Gardening in the Shade* (1964), *Ground Cover Plants* (1964), *A Flower for Every Day* (1965), *Carefree Gardening* (1966) and *Gardening on Clay and Lime* (1970). She had also contributed to *The Oxford Book of Garden Flowers* and *The Shell Book of Gardens*.

She did not consciously set about creating a nursery – it was a natural evolution from growing so many plants so well. Her gardening style was becoming widely copied, and the demand for plants from her garden became insatiable; her eye for a good plant was faultless, and she shared her plants readily. Her double dark red carnation and the

East Lambrook Manor

Korean chrysanthemum Innocence are still good hardy plants today. The small crimson daisy with a large yellow centre that she had from Ireland and mentioned in *Cottage Garden Flowers* still exists in gardens. By 1964 her list contained 11 campanulas, 13 euphorbias and 15 grasses, but nearly 60 cultivars of primroses.

Primroses were probably her favourite plants. Not only did she seek out the older forms of double-flowering, hose-in-hose, and Jack-in-the-green primroses, but she grew and named some coloured single forms of her own raising, including Lambrook Yellow, Lilac, Peach, Crimson and Pink. 'No other flowers seem quite so much at home in the cottage garden as does the primrose. It cannot help enjoying itself in that packed damp atmosphere, with shelter from the house, of taller plants and plentiful libations of washing-up water and mulchings with tea leaves'.

She exchanged plants of her rare double forms with the leading primrose growers of the day throughout the British Isles. William Chalmers of Stonehaven, Mary McMurtrie of Balbithan, Mrs Emerson of Limavady and Tony Venison were all recipients. The double pink *juliae* primrose she sent to William Chalmers is still listed by his son David Chalmers today. She never attempted the hybridisation

of double primroses which would have been possible by growing the pollen-bearing polyanthus Prince Silverwings, although she grew hose-in-hose primroses from seed; only single primroses left the garden with the Lambrook name attached.

Margery Fish's own cultivars, known or listed, are:

> *Artemesia absinthium* Lambrook Silver; Lambrook Giant
> *Astrantia major* Margery Fish
> *Euphorbia wulfenii Lambrook Gold*
> *Dianthus* Lambrook Beauty
> *Hebe* Margery Fish
> *Pentstemon* Margery Fish
> *Polemonium carneum* Lambrook Mauve; Lambrook Pink
> *Primula vulgaris* Lambrook Crimson; Lambrook Ivory
>   Lambrook Peach; Lambrook Pink; Lambrook Yellow
> *Pulmonaria saccharata* Margery Fish
> *Santolina* Lambrook Variety

Her enthusiasm lasted until her death in 1969, and she ensured the survival of her garden by leaving her estate to her nephew Henry Boyd-Carpenter, who until the death of his father maintained the garden and expanded the nursery into its present form.

The garden has suffered, as so many plantsmen's gardens suffer on the death of the owner, from the loss of many of the rare cottage cultivars of which she had written. Her education of a generation of gardeners has however encouraged people who have those plants to return them to their original homes in her garden; a visit is always full of interest for the enthusiast.

Her gardening is particularly remembered for its use of cottage-garden plants; but this represented only one aspect. By finding hardy plants from botanical gardens throughout the British Isles which she succeeded in growing and flowering out of season in shade on heavy clay she extended the uses of attractive ground cover. The garden changed subtly in her later years. After 1960 her fame was still growing, and she visited ever more gardens. She slowly began to grow more trees and shrubs, with fewer small herbaceous plants.

The kindness and generosity she extended to all visitors meant the widening circle of her friends was a means of giving and distributing

The cowhouse and the barton had their lines softened by sympathetic planting

rare English garden plants. Once her impetus disappeared only the emergence of the National Society for the Conservation of Plants and Gardens filled the gap which was left.

After Andrew Norton bought East Lambrook from Henry Boyd-Carpenter in 1975 he found her notes on a few other people's gardens in a drawer in the Malthouse. They had never been published – were not intended for publication – but the features she enjoyed in gardens indicate that an even greater change would have come to the planting at East Lambrook had she survived a further ten years. (The notes are published as an Appendix at the end of this book).

For the last ten years English gardening has been so concerned with preservation and conservation it has missed the spur of original thought. How would our gardens be today had a good communicator of new ideas propounded them in the face of our present obsession with the past? How many small fish ponds and fountains would have become shady streams and pools under Margery's guidance? Her importance as a gardener, and communicator, made others follow in the direction she led: to use well-grown effective plants to create the type of garden which the world comes to the British Isles to see.

2

The Making of the Garden

By 1954–55, Margery was writing her first book, she had become well known as a lecturer, and for her many magazine and newspaper features on gardening. Her sister, Mrs Boyd-Carpenter, felt that this book *We Made A Garden*, would have been better titled 'How I Made a Garden for Walter'. It was indeed something of a tribute to him, and reflects that after his death, she was lonely and had time on her hands. She had memories of some very happy years, and the increasing success of her articles in *The Field* and *Amateur Gardening* made her feel that a lasting record of the restoration and creation of the garden at East Lambrook Manor would interest a worthwhile number of people. She remembered her early training with Lord Northcliffe never to use two words when one will do, and fell to work.

The book reveals her original intention to make a garden as unpretentious as the house, but one that could contain crooked paths and unexpected corners; to this day, every visitor walking round wonders constantly 'What shall I find next?' It had to be easy to run, because for the first two years after buying East Lambrook they still lived in London, and left it to take care of itself for long periods. This is what may have taught Walter never to rely on flowers: a garden needs a good bone structure, and intelligent use of evergreens, to be clothed all through the year. Flowers would then be an added pleasure. One of Margery's most quoted remarks was 'If I ever hear of a good garden I visit it in winter, and if I like it return in the summer'. Hers was never an about-to-be or just-had-been garden. Walter expected it to be like the house, always ready for the unexpected guest.

East Lambrook Manor is long, low and built of honey-coloured stone. Not much garden was originally attached to the house, but Margery and Walter bought some outbuildings and an orchard, which added a further two acres. For the future this was promising, but for the present it added difficulties to implementing their idea that houses and gardens should look an entity, as if they had grown up together.

The garden with the house was divided at the back into two small plots with walls and grass – a legacy from the time when the house was two cottages. As in all good Somerset farmhouses there was a barton or farmyard area where the horses walked to turn the cider press. Between these two plots and the barton another wall further divided the area. Beneath all these walls banks had been made and vertical stones added. It was obvious the walls and stones must be cleared and piled up for the future.

A high wall which screened from the road was finished in the local rough stone. Walter suggested that work should begin at the top of the wall while they planned the rest of the garden. Margery bought some easy rock plants from a local nursery, and sowed seeds of alyssum and valerian; she would clamber up the heaps of stones to water them. Slowly the stones disappeared by the cartload to farmers who would fetch them. In later years she was amazed to have to buy in many, many more than they gave away at the beginning. Nonetheless the removal of the stones allowed them to visualise how the place could look. Clearance of the barton was essential because of its central position between the house and outbuildings. A bonfire burned for weeks and the scrap metal seemed endless. There was then no rubbish collection and as a quick means of disposal Walter had holes dug in out-of-the-way places and all the rubbish buried. Later, after Walter's death, when more of the land was taken into the garden, she came across these tips and cleared them by the regular refuse removals.

The two walls between the barton and the orchard were used to take the heavy rubbish; Walter covered it all and created a rock garden. Its completion coincided with the visit of the first real gardeners they had received, who informed her that the large stones were all in at the wrong angle and heavy rains would result in the soil being washed away from them. Eventually a cousin replaced them for her, and with few rock plants and little experience, they grew annuals in the profusion most people do in their first gardening season. These rock gardens eventually became the first raised beds in the garden, as they filled with hyssop, penstemon, and small shrubs such as ceratostigma and potentillas.

Walter saw the potential of these beds, and decided flat stones were more generous than gravel. Between these stones were a few Dresden China daisies, which enjoyed the cool root-run; their abundant flowers in this situation created the first effect for which East Lambrook was to

become famous. Walter was never keen on small plants, but these daisies were the exception, and he wanted every flowering tree surrounded with them. They remained one of Margery's favourites. Splitting up the 'hen and chickens' daisies of the Stuart herbals was to remain her panacea in times of stress.

THE BACK GARDEN

When the time came to design the back garden, Walter's principles were again given every consideration: the bigger the lawn, the more spacious the garden; one long bed holds as many plants as four small spots, and avoids the restlessness of brown smudges on green. Walter was equally firm over paths, conscious that paths which are too narrow make the garden lose proportion. He liked breadth, generosity and a feeling of space in both house and garden, but above all the elimination of unnecessary detail.

Making the garden become part of the house was easier than in many projects of this type, as it could be built round the house. The construction of the house helped, as the big door in the hall where they usually sat opened directly to the garden. The hall was paved with flagstones, and they paved the garden outside on the same level: it was difficult to tell where one began and the other ended. The front garden too was paved, and the only way to reach the back was through the house or round by the road. In the winter a wood fire smouldered on the open hearth, giving a convenient supply of potash and charcoal for garden operations.

Walter insisted the lawn should run nearly up to the house, leaving only a narrow bed for perennials and climbers to clothe the wall. A variegated sycamore in the lawn near the house gave an established air. But for the first time in Walter's gardening life he realised that making a lawn was not all quick decisions like running a newspaper. He made simple mistakes, which could have been avoided given time and care. However, once a lawn is planted and regularly cut, it requires little attention. Having piles of rough hamstone, Walter used this to build

Walter preferred flower beds level with the grass and path. Here on the terraces, *Verbascum brousa*, *Atriplex hortensis cupreata*, and *Echinops ritro* dominate

a rough low drystone wall between the lawn and what was to be the drive. It fascinated Margery, and she repeated it in other parts of the garden, using every crevice for alpines. Walter was pleased with her efforts, but eventually lost patience, telling her she spent too much time poking belly-crawlers into rat-holes!

'PERFECT LAWNS, PATHS, HEDGES AND WALLS'

The grass was cut regularly, and edges trimmed, a gully between lawn and wall leaving room for the mower. During Walter's lifetime she felt that his assertion that her flowers did not matter was unjust. Later on she came to realise, though, that his four rules of a good garden are true priorities: perfect lawns, paths, hedges and walls. As she became more experienced and confident as a gardener she often remarked on the beauty of a formal garden of grass and shaped trees, and would express disappointment at wonderful plants, both rare and exotic, being ruined by the lack of Walter's principles around them. Walter would no more leave the grass uncut than not shave. He liked flowers if they were properly grown, but he looked at a garden as a whole, never at the perfection of one plant.

To satisfy Walter's ideas of perfection in making paths was a further source of concern. He considered that nothing could beat a good gravel path and it should be rolled so hard nothing would spoil the surface, nor any weed find a foothold. To turn the barton into a well-made drive large enough for a dozen cars was not easy. Visitors to the garden can still see a substantial slope from the Malthouse to the gate. By levelling and removing almost a foot of clay, the base was made substantially hard. In this type of path and drive the edges matter most, as they take the least traffic and make the easiest home for weeds. After Walter's death the struggle against weeds was lost, as Margery ceased the applications of weedkillers. Eventually the main drive was surfaced with a bituminous product, and the other paths paved. The paving at the back of the house and the path that led to the barton were levelled into a rubble base, and sealed with cement in the cracks. The cracks widened, and ever avid for somewhere fresh to plant thymes, pinks and Dresden China daisies, Margery filled them with small cuttings. They needed the occasional

weeding – as Walter had always said they would.

Having completed access to the major part of the garden, Walter decided the walls needed clothing, particularly the end of the house where the old stones were too decayed to be repaired and had once had a stucco covering. Together they bought roses, pyracantha, cotoneaster and clematis. Walter preferred blue *Clematis jackmanii*: when sent for six, she bought the red Ville de Lyon for herself. Walter made a magnificent show with the *jackmanii*, but not for three years did he help hers to grow. Clematis are difficult to train, and after a period she decided to grow them on wire netting over low walls in the Victorian manner so each flower could be individually looked down on.

The roses on the front of the house grew luxuriantly, Mme Abel Chatenay and Lady Hillingdon being trained over the windows. Paul's Scarlet and climbing General McArthur looked magnificent against the yellow hamstone. While waiting for them to make their effect Walter bought a collection of hunting trophies to cover the bare walls.

After Walter's death the ampelopsis grew too big and Margery cut them down. Passion flowers and *Forsythia suspensa* went up other walls. Walter disliked wisterias because they took too long to flower, but eventually Margery planted two – and a bigonia – all three were unsuccessful. She then planted a *Chimonanthus fragrans* Luteus which gave her great pleasure. Her love of green flowers made her plant a stauntonia and on the north wall *Garrya elliptica*, using the bushy honeysuckle *Lonicera fragrantissima* for further winter flowers. Phygelius species were grateful for the protection of the walls. She was then pioneering by planting *Eucalyptus gunnii*, not thought to be very hardy, for the decorative effect of its leaves.

After clothing the walls Walter turned his methodical attention to hedges. He decided that vigorous growth and camouflage of unwelcome views were necessary. Despite their friends' advice, the quickest and greenest hedge then available, *Cypressus macrocarpa*, was selected. Gardeners say it gets established and dies, and this was true at East Lambrook. After Walter's death, *Lonicera nitida* was planted inside the cupressus, to replace it. All the smaller hedges in the garden came from *Lonicera nitida* cuttings given by the Boyd-Carpenters. Margery found this the easiest material for hedges, as it shaped like yew, could be used for topiary, and could even make an edging like box; with a fairly long life, it looked in keeping in most situations. Later she experimented

The lawn and the house from the green gate show that perfect lawns and perfect paths make a good garden

with lavender and santolina for clipped hedges, and fuchsias and *Kerria japonica* for naturally flowering hedges, but never achieved such a satisfactory effect. Only in the orchard did she persuade Walter to overcome his dislike of the brown leaves of a beech hedge. Despite his grumbling he eventually became quite fond of the beech there, where he did not want quickthorn and the price of yew would have been prohibitive.

THE TERRACE GARDEN

Once the hedges were completed and the lawn and drive made, Walter conceded Margery could set to work in what had always been considered her part of the garden. By this time she was becoming increasingly confident she could grow difficult plants well. With this

confidence she viewed the area which was to become the terrace garden. Walter assumed simply that she would grow flowers; she herself wanted nothing formal, just something simple and cottagey to go with the long-low house.

The ground rises away from the lower lawn, and the slope is terraced. This change of levels meant the path to the orchard must be slightly curving. For the first level she made low stone steps with high walls to retain the earth. Walter gravelled the wide paths which gave a feeling of space; after his death they were paved as a spacious terrace. She then decided to raise up the garden each side of the path with a series of terraces, each supported by a low wall, in which to grow small rockery plants. This is the most difficult planting to make attractive: the easiest is a single border to a wall, the second a double border. But this series of borders needed to look well from four angles, and still combine with borders at the front and behind. There were three terraces to the left, three to the right, and here a fourth triangular bed had to taper in to fill the space. Walter considered the whole effect foolish, and asked her when she would construct the grand canyon. By the early spring, however, remarks like 'Stones, stones, stones', or 'How is the floral quarry this morning?' ceased and it was virtually completed.

Walter in fact secretly admired her energy and persistence in the task and the day she was ready to plant, he said 'Now we will put in the pole roses'. Pole roses were the suburban dream of the Daily Mail Ideal Home Exhibition between the wars, and the last thing she wanted. She had hoped for low-growing plants to give a tapestry effect, with taller plants at the back and sides. But by widening the path, winding up between the beds, pole roses were duly inserted. Cupid, a small shell-pink variation of the golden Mermaid, was planted, with Chaplin's Pink, climbing Lady Hillingdon – for its brilliant crimson foliage in spring – Gloire de Dijon, William Allen Richardson, General McArthur, and Paul's Scarlet.

3

Learning Walter's Principles

Margery admitted that she learnt much from Walter during their first year of gardening – probably mostly in terms of judging the potential of a proposed design. She was a novice and assumed he was too, but as the year progressed she realised that having employed professional gardeners in the past he had absorbed their wisdom, and saw their follies. She remembered in later life her feeling of horror that he could take a knife to some chrysanthemums potted for the winter, because he felt that the gardener in question was neglecting the rest of the garden; but she remembered also never to devote too much time to the things she liked best at the expense of the rest of the garden.

Walter's views on the level of the flower beds differed from hers, however. He preferred them to be level with the grass and path, not raised, as he felt that a bed made flush with the path or lawn looks larger and more attractive. In later years she became more enthusiastic over the idea, planting sprawling plants near the path to soften the line. At the outset Margery put stones vertically at the edges of all the beds, leaving 2–3in protruding; later Walter told her the effect was pleasanter and equally effective if the stones were laid flat: something was needed to separate the flower beds from the path, but the edging should not distract attention from the flowers.

This theory made bricks and tiles superfluous; little box hedges, with London pride, thrift or *Gentiana acaulis*, were more in keeping. Later in her gardening she experimented with bergenia, *Stachys lanata* and once with acanthus, but her preference was for mossy saxifrage and daisies.

Walter took little interest in how the flower beds were planted in the formative period of Margery's gardening life, though she was urged to use the occasional tall plant in the front of the beds to break monotony. After using lupins, Walter liked groups of iris for their clean upward sweep. He also advised on the importance of massed effects, so instead of one delphinium she planted six, to avoid a spotty effect.

The main lessons she learned from Walter in those early years were

The path to the privy. 'Plant firmly, and never grow a feeble plant', were Walter's rules, but Margery softened the line with sprawling plants near the path

to plant firmly and never to grow a feeble plant. She would often find a row of sick plants, lying pulled out, looking like dead rats. Walter was a good teacher and a hard taskmaster, and planting came first in their lives. No plant should stay out of the ground a minute longer than necessary; heeling plants in was not good enough. Planting too closely was something Walter would not tolerate. At certain stages of the garden's development he would deliberately plant a shrub too many to fill up, but not often. Walter felt that however small the plant it had all the world to grow in, and Margery would hastily fill the gap with her annuals, which at the end of the summer were merely material for the compost heap.

As the first summer wore on she grew restive at Walter's repeated comment that 'It is nice to walk in a garden, but better still to take a hoe'. This never seemed correct, and as the years passed she decided secateurs were what was needed. A snip in time saves nine became her response, because she saw how easily an overhanging branch and a few dead heads could be removed on her morning walks. The style of gardening for which East Lambrook became famous, in which the

larger plants protected the smaller throughout the season, made fresh green wood essential. Simple biennials like Canterbury bells will give three successive flowering seasons if they are deadheaded; naturalised daffodils do not quickly deteriorate, if free of other pests. Some half-hardy shrubs and plants ripen their wood in autumn much more if deadheaded quickly, and then tolerate more frost in the winter. Always an original, she sharpened an old sword and deadheaded in rapid time. Walter boasted about a noble owner of his acquaintance who said no dead flower could ever be found in his garden, deadheaded with secateurs, and dropped the remains. Margery said she was not the fifth gardener, and would not clear up after him. Eventually it became a joke, and at lunchtime she would be told where the fifth gardener could work that afternoon.

One essential was never be sentimental about a plant because one flower is left on it – better to sacrifice the flower, and make a good job of cutting down the plant, especially with lupins and delphiniums, where the reward is a second crop of flowers. Walter's strong views on watering were also followed; nothing irritated him more than to be told 'You cannot start watering unless you go on doing it every day'. His theory was that these people did not do it properly anyway. He had lengths of hose to reach every part of the garden, and would take several days to do the job as he thought it should be done. Only on the lawn was a sprinkler permissible. A strong jet must be directed for several minutes at the foot of every plant. In later life one of Margery's fondest memories of him was as he watered the plants, wearing an old panama hat, short-sleeved shirt and waistcoat – keeping the garden going for a good fortnight, as he said.

THE COMPOST HEAP

After the war, as water shortages developed, they mulched more of the garden and kept the top soil loose, but by this time she had built up the fertility of the soil. She created a routine of first compost for roses, second for clematis and, with her growing need of colour for every day, a good mulch for the dahlias if the compost would run to it. In their early years the heavy clay soil needed every improvement possible, and even later they found that composting was

almost as important as actually gardening. Margery eventually settled for a recipe she obtained from an American book – the only instance where she drew on a transatlantic source for gardening ideas. First she put all waste green vegetation in a heap to which she added household refuse until the heap was brown. She would then combine this with any other suitable material and leave it to stand once more. The final heap was made in four layers, repeated until all the material was used up: firstly a layer of her rotted compost, then an equal depth of farmyard manure, then this was covered with earth, and finally it was thickly dusted with wood ash. Pipes were inserted vertically into the heap as it was built, for ventilation. Later the earth was changed to sand, finishing with grass tufts from the vegetable garden to seal the heap and let the heat kill the weed-seeds; occasionally old straw and sawdust were used in place of sand. The entire heap was hidden by *Lonicera nitida* and she would collect the liquid manure oozing out in cans rather than let it drain to the hedge.

RETHINKING

After the summer of 1939 Walter and Margery let the house for a year. Walter became Press Advisor to the Censor and Margery went with him to London as his secretary. Their return to East Lambrook was a shock. The family who hired the house had kept the grass kempt, but everywhere else was a mass of undergrowth, nowhere worse than the terrace garden. Nothing was staked, and the height and untidiness dwarfed the low house below.

Walter was horrified at the chaos. A friend, Malcolm Keen, asked Margery if she had ever thought of getting professional help from landscape gardeners. She said no, but he attacked again, talking about Elizabethan gardens, and soon had Walter's interest. The result was that the pole roses in the terrace garden disappeared, to be replaced by the shapely cypress *Chamaecyparis lawsoniana* Fletcheri. These trees were clipped each August and became a famous feature of the terrace garden: 'Margery's pudding trees', as the family called them, showed the importance of including some evergreens in every garden scheme.

On each side of steep steps leading to the higher part of the garden Irish yews gave accent. Tall conifers can freely clothe a bare wall, and

even rock gardens could, in Margery's view, be improved by the use of slow-growing dwarf ones. Variegated euonymus and choisya gave green when all was bare; hedges too contributed. If a garden had this definite bone structure, it kept its character at all seasons.

THE DITCH GARDEN

An interesting feature of East Lambrook was the water garden, created because the ditch boundary against the orchard was always full of running water. The orchard was bought with the idea of making a 'wild' garden with banks tamed and planted, preserving only the willows. But after the ditch was widened, and flat stones put down for pools and waterfalls, the water disappeared. At least that made the whole area become more accessible. It formed a perfect backdrop, with lumps of hamstone for the east-facing bank, for her rarer primroses and polyanthus. She had a small collection of alpine and native strawberries on the other side, while a wide border of clay was removed to make a moist garden where Asiatic primulas grew beneath the trees.

At the back of the Malthouse, the original boundary turned sharply right for the water to drain away at the far side of the garden. It seemed an ideal corner for more stonework. Margery and Walter terraced the ground and made shallow steps down to the stream. On the other side was a little paved court with steep steps up to the orchard. Round the corner they scooped out more clay and made a wide paved wall with hamstone tiles. Primulas, *Iris kaempferi* and *Meconopsis baileyii* (*betonicifolia*) were grown here in an unrestrained manner reminiscent of Mrs Clive Ponsonby Fane at Brympton d'Evercy, near Yeovil, an important later influence on her gardening. On the orchard side large stones were set up the bank and sun-loving zauschneria, sternbergia, rock roses and androsace were planted. Walter constructed a wall down the steepest part. He laid drainage pipes across the orchard and arranged big stones over which the water would tumble to the stream below – but no water ever came. This piece of garden, which they called the Lido, was dry! In the end Margery planted Asiatic primulas in what should have been the river bed, after digging out more clay and adding sand and peat. Bartley Miller and Postford hybrid primulas grew to perfection with their feet in the clay and heads in the sun.

HOMES FOR ALPINE TREASURES

Eventually two rock gardens were constructed. After Margery visited Ireland she appreciated the gardening that Gladys Emerson did at The Leeke, Limavady and Miss Wynne at Avoca: rock gardens were suitable planting places for their laced pinks, and rarer forms of hedgerow flowers. The first rock garden, or as Margery termed it home for alpine treasures, was expedient rather than intentional. She and Walter felt few gardens lent themselves to a 'few stones rising self-consciously in a lawn', thinking these were as bad as a Victorian rockery, constructed of burr and concrete in a dark corner where only ferns could grow. The two rocky beds against the walls of the barton were excellent for Margery's treasures. The 'Coliseum' was born because they had to dig out the clay soil that had silted the west end of the house. They discovered the remains of a fireplace behind the present chimney. This solved the problem of how to support the ground which was several feet above the level of the foundations. On each side of the fireplace they made a series of steps and Walter instructed Margery about what she could plant to relieve the hard angular lines. With few plants to choose from she used a stonecrop (*Sedum spurium*) and every year pulled out barrowloads for the compost heap. An even greater error was the introduction of *Helxine soleirolii* (mind-your-own-business). She thought it more attractive than stonecrop, but eventually planted creeping thymes to cover the dry, sunny areas of broken wall.

After the completion of the terraced garden, and more walls to play with, she developed a range of wall plants. Single and double aubretia were grown from seed, arabis, *Dianthus caesius* and rock campanulas were used in variety. She planted saxifrages and gypsophila to foam over the stones, *Saponaria ocymoides* and geraniums on the top of the walls and in crevices. On a rough wall round the lawn grew rock roses, androsaces, aethionemas and shrubby thymes, brightened in spring by mounds of *Alyssum saxatile* in orange and lemon – two colours that were contrasted in her hose-in-hose polyanthus. She added lavenders and silver plants, with cheiranthus and erysimums. Again she grew creeping thyme in dry places. At the base of the walls she planted various primroses: many varieties are sadly lost, though three of her favourites, Kinlough Beauty, Jill and E.R. Janes, are still available.

THE FRONT OF THE HOUSE

In front of the house there was only a narrow strip of ground, originally covered with laurels. These were dug out, and they levelled the ground and laid crazy paving with over-wide cracks between the stones. The cracks were planted generously but that did not stop the weeds, so Walter insisted on it all coming up; Margery however persevered until he eventually allowed her a few areas for planting. Both found it far too tidy on completion. Blue stone had been used for paving, as they had not realised the possibilities of hamstone. Though valerian was planted on top of the walls and colourful alpines in them, it remained cheerless. The concrete soon deteriorated, and with help from the crowbar, more plants were added to the scene.

The importance of the paved garden is that once again neither Margery nor Walter turned their backs upon a suburban idea because it was at that time unfashionable. Her planting became a byword for good plantsmanship. She used all the creeping thymes she could get: *Thymus serpyllum* Annie Hall, Pink Chintz and Coccineus, *Thymus lanuginosus* in grey mats, and humps of *Thymus ericaefolius* in bronze. *Iris pumila* was used in white, blue, purple and primrose shades, and *Sisyrinchium bermudianum* planted for its dainty grassy foliage with the larger *Sisyrinchium striatum*. Crimson shading came from *Dianthus deltoides*, while the local Cheddar pink *Dianthus caesius* covered a large area with its scented flowers. She used the prostrate blue veronica for floor covering and included the pink Mrs Holt and Silver Queen for clarity, the woolly grey-green *Veronica pectinata Rosea*, and *Veronica amoena* with threadlike foliage and light blue speedwell flowers.

Campanula carpatica is good in untrampled paving, and they planted blue Isabel, wedgwood-blue Opal and White Star. *Helichrysum bellidioides*, with *Antennaria dioica*, Alba and Rosea were used, and into the carpet she mixed aizoon saxifrages with erodiums and globularia, and frankenia for its pink stemless flowers in July and August. With *Raoulia australis*, *glabra* and *lutescens*, this planting made mats covering the surfaces of the stones. Margery's favourite creeping mint was *Mentha requienii*, much to be preferred to pennyroyal, *Mentha pulegium*. This packed mass of plants gave great pleasure on two scores. Firstly she had no formal botanical training and learnt her plantings by trial and

error, and secondly she particularly enjoyed the colour schemes she could weave by adding her beloved daisies for the spring.

Around the narrow beds of the paved garden Walter planted climbing roses, and the 'fifth gardener' added *Clematis henryi* Alba and the Rose of White and pale pink King George V. There was not room enough for a selection of flowers throughout the year. Walter liked blue hydrangeas, Margery liked pink, and after his death she filled these beds with pink hydrangeas and pentstemons, using *Helleborus orientalis* and *foetidus* to flower out of season. On the south side of the paved garden she planted her most tender bulbs – freesias, nerines, *Amaryllis belladonna* and agapanthus, even occasionally scented *Acidanthera bicolor* Murielae.

Herbs grew by the back door near the kitchen, particularly the everyday ones. Both she and Walter felt that a full herb garden needs space, and like a Victorian posy must be trim to be effective. She was not the first gardener to use bergamot, salvia, hyssop, rue and fennel for their decorative effect in the flower garden, but she was the first to make them a standby in her round-the-year planting. Eleanour Sinclair Rohde with her wider historical knowledge had interested an earlier generation in Elizabethan herbs. Margery drew on her ideas for her decorative effect.

With the completion of the herb garden the garden was designed to their satisfaction, and she was left to develop the planting along the lines she wished – provided it did not conflict with Walter's idea of a well-planted garden. He repeated with relish the story of a cousin who when asked when he would complete his garden replied 'Never, I hope'.

4

Influences on Planting

Margery considered her family had been forbearing towards her. Before she married she left gardening to her sisters, preferring to go off to golf, saying that gardeners were fools to keep working and not enjoying their garden: 'Why have a lovely garden if you never have time to sit in it and enjoy it?' Once married and drawn into it, she felt her lack of botanical training or even basic knowledge of horticulture was a considerable drawback. In fact it was not; her mind was usefully free from other gardeners' habits. But Margery never understood this, and felt inferior when with better-trained but less capable or imaginative gardeners.

Once the structure of the garden was completed, her idea was to give it as long a season as possible. This received no encouragement from Walter, who wanted a brilliant display when the sun shone. It was wartime, and travel and access to new sources of plants were limited. Margery became an avid reader of good gardening and horticultural literature, and also kept her eyes open to the plants she saw growing in the local cottage gardens. She records her first find of some double white primroses and of exchanging half a pound of tea for them during wartime rationing. By using her contacts in Fleet Street, she acquired a substantial library at the end of the war. Reading these and articles by gardeners such as Vita Sackville-West and George Morrison Taylor, Margery commenced to plan her planting away from the accepted mores of her time. 'Our gardening ways are changing. Instead of trying to make our gardens as different as possible from nature we now strive for a natural effect, and aim at producing in the garden what nature does outside, but with cultivated plants', she wrote much later (*Carefree Gardening*).

MRS C.W. EARLE

Among the greatest influences on gardening this century is the little known Mrs C.W. Earle, born Maria Theresa Villers in 1836.

Dried flowers in the dining room. Margery first lectured on flower arranging locally, and gradually introduced her ideas into the garden

A poor relation of the Earl of Clarendon, she was the eldest daughter of the famed beauty Elizabeth Charlotte Liddell. Shortage of money after her father's death meant she travelled extensively in Italy. She eventually married Charles Earle: one of her two younger twin sisters married Lord Lock, the other, Edith, married Bulwer Lytton in 1864.

Mrs Earle did not garden seriously until 1876, and then recalled the old cottage gardens of her childhood in Hertfordshire, and also the Renaissance gardens of Italy. She added to these ideas those she learnt from Ruskin – she had been his pupil at the Slade School of Art. An admirer of the pre-Raphaelites, she created a pre-Raphaelite-style garden which Morris and the Arts & Crafts movement applauded.

In 1897 she wrote *Pot Pourri from a Surrey Garden*, recording much of her life and garden work. She was helped in this by her niece Lady Constance Lytton, and the book became the first-ever bestseller on gardening, running through many editions. The formula was repeated as *More Pot Pourri* in 1899, a third *Pot Pourri* in

1903 and once more in 1914, with Ethel Case, as *Pot Pourri Mixed by Two*.

By her sister's marriage into the Lytton family she became the aunt of Edwin Lutyens – she was always known as Aunt T. Many of the ideas she had gleaned from her visits to Italian gardens were introduced into her conversations and writing. She was also a plantswoman of some skill – as befitted a kinswoman of John Gerard, via the Russells of Chippenham Park, Cambridgeshire. A record of her conversations with Edwin Lutyens would have been inspirational to Margery.

Mrs Earle's writing became most influential; she was the first contributor to *Garden Colour in Spring, Summer and Winter* (1905), and Gertrude Jekyll copied the idea, writing her own *Colour in the Flower Garden* in 1908. The relationship between Mrs Earle, Miss Jekyll and Edwin Lutyens was complex, sometimes cool, sometimes friendly, but I believe that the great garden of Hestercombe in Somerset was designed by Lutyens and Jekyll as their private memorial to her ideas.

Mrs Earle's use of colour in the garden to create the illusion of mystery, depth and distance was an important influence in the overall effect that Margery started to create between 1949 and 1954. Here are some extracts from her contribution to *The Century Book of Gardening*, written probably in 1900 after the public success of *Pot Pourri from a Surrey Garden*.

SHRUB BORDERS AND HARDY FLOWERS

For such herbaceous borders to be beautiful they would have to be planted in a very bold manner, with large masses of colour, and this means broad bands of earth more or less covered with manure for six or eight months of the year. This would be anything but attractive. A wide mixed border if not on the simple dotted cottage system, should be intersected with plants which are good in form and restful in colour and are much the same all the year round; besides, many flowers and plants do so badly in full sun.

We hear much in these days of herbaceous borders, often described in poetical language, and which are supposed to grow all the flowers of the year in the utmost perfection, mentioning in a light and airy way that the Christmas Rose may be picked in the depth of winter,

and the Violet may flourish from November to April. All this is really book gardening or newspaper gardening. There is nothing so difficult as keeping the same borders in perfection during eight or nine months of the year. To obtain that result, the herbaceous border can only be an enlargement of the English cottage garden which needs nothing but loving care – filling up bare places as they occur by the constant introduction of fresh plants, whether perennial, annual, or half hardy; watering plants as they come into bud, thinning out vigorously when necessary, mulching during the hot summer days, and covering with manure the bare earth in winter.

Mystery being one of the great beauties of a fair sized garden, there is no reason why special spaces should not be concealed in such a way that their period of rest should not offend the eye. Miss Jekyll's description of her herbaceous border is most interesting (in *Wood and Garden*) as it is planted with the idea of good effects of both form and colour; but this is only for a comparatively limited time in the year, her spring flowers and many of her autumn ones being kept entirely apart and grown in appropriate places. A very perfect herbaceous border may be had in the spring, when most things are more or less low growing, the beautiful Crown Imperials being the great exception; but to my mind the spring garden, with its numerous interesting bulbs, should more or less be a garden on its own fading off into a wood.

To get the border to look bright in May, June and September is easy enough; the great difficulty is to keep it beautiful through July and August.

ELEANOUR SINCLAIR ROHDE

Margery was also influenced by a writer of a later generation, Eleanour Sinclair Rohde, born at Allepy in India in 1881. At St Hilda's, Oxford, where in those days no degrees were given to women, she decided to research gardening, working among the early leech books and herbals. Her books *The Old English Gardening Books* and *Old English Herbals* represent the opening of the world of Elizabethan and Stuart gardens to the uneducated gardener. In 1931 she published *The Scented Garden*, a forerunner for her most important work on gardening, *Gardens*

of Delight, in 1934: the title was taken from John Parkinson's great gardening book of 1629, *Paradisi in Sole*. This book stimulated Margery throughout her gardening life.

Eleanour Sinclair Rohde was not the first to write on the winter garden, but she was the first to record the opinion that when the history of gardening during this century was written, the interest in winter-flowering plants would be the most remarkable fact to emerge. For the last twenty years of her life she kept a nursery at her garden, Cranham Lodge, Reigate, selling the herbs of which she had written. She designed both herb and bee gardens, and died after a strenuous lecture tour in America in 1950.

Margery was fascinated, too, by Eleanour Sinclair Rohde's knowledge of her old garden plants. This stimulated her search for plants of the past three centuries which had been forgotten in the blaze of pelargoniums, calceolarias, lobelias and salvias during the last fifty years.

ROBINSON & JEKYLL

William Robinson and Gertrude Jekyll were more popular gardening writers, and some of their ideas were in sympathy with hers. Margery did not entertain the idea of a William Robinson wild garden: 'natural' possibly, but plants left unattended died. Having no children of her own Margery was maternal with her plants. She did enjoy Robinson's book *The English Flower Garden*, referring to it if she discovered a garden cultivar she could not name.

Her absorption of the ideas in the books of Gertrude Jekyll was patchy to say the least. A dictum of hers was that English gardens were over-rosed and over-rhododendroned – a view in contrast to Miss Jekyll's. She was particularly attached to gold-laced polyanthus and florists' pinks, two plants which Miss Jekyll, who abhorred florists' flowers as artificial, totally condemned. Nor did Margery ever plant her walls in the style described in the Jekyll book *Wall and Water Gardens*. But Miss Jekyll, using the pre-Raphaelite view of garden colour, did have some indirect influence on East Lambrook plants; Margery was frequently heard to say 'Miss Jekyll was right, as usual'.

East Lambrook Manor

Vita Sackville-West

Vita Sackville-West was probably the writer of Margery's own time who inspired her use of planting for garden effect. It was a two-way relationship: Vita, in need of recreation or inspiration, would often travel down the gardens on either side of the A30. This would include Stourhead, famous for its landscape, as well as a visit to Mrs Clive Ponsonby Fane at Brympton d'Evercy and Phyllis Reiss at Tintinhull. All gardeners know that good ideas and good plants are easily interchanged. There was no overlapping and rivalry of scholarship between these two great ladies of the garden; their interests ran parallel. Where Vita produced a grand garden of display, Margery liked the cottage-garden flowers of previous centuries. These interested but did not fascinate Vita, who always enjoyed Margery's writing but never considered her an equal. Her review of *We Made a Garden* in the *Observer* was 'Crammed with good advice. I defy any amateur gardener not to find pleasure, encouragement and profit from *We Made a Garden*' – praise enough for Margery, who twenty years earlier had never gardened. The ideas of Vita Sackville-West seem to have been discussed by Margery, Mrs Clive and Phyllis Reiss – as evidenced by the close friendliness obtained at East Lambrook by growing good plants well in complete harmony with each other.

E. A. Bowles

Of all her gardening acquaintances she probably learnt most from, enjoyed most, the great plantsman E.A. Bowles. Born in 1865 he was an old man when Margery first met him, and his garden at Myddelton House, Enfield, was declining; he realised that she was a plantswoman who could care for his treasures after his demise, which came in 1954.

A view of part of the ditch, with hostas, primulas, rogersia and ulmaria

East Lambrook Manor, with the *Acer pseudoplatanus leopoldii variegata* that made Margery Fish decide to buy the house. In the foreground is *Centranthus ruber*, (red valerian)

Flowers on the hall table. The influence of Constance Spry was always present in Margery's flower arrangements

She had read his three great gardening classics, *My Garden in Spring, My Garden in Summer, My Garden in Autumn and Winter*, first published in 1914. Bowles instilled in her his love of plant eccentricities – double flowers, coloured bracts, variegated foliage or even historical association. The two areas of his garden that most interested her were what he called 'Tom Tiddler's ground', with its mass of variegated-leafed plants, but especially 'the lunatic asylum', where his plant freaks grew. Here Margery saw the type of plants she could transpose back to East Lambrook to help create a garden which would give both an immediate visual impact, and the feeling of mystery, of wondering whatever plant one would see next.

Mr Bowles' garden and his immense knowledge of his wide range of plants made her discuss among her friends the use of ground-cover plants. She was gardening at a time when however wealthy the gardener, trained help was not available. Her problem was to keep down weeds in a garden of increasing fertility, and to keep as many species and cultivars as possible happy in confined spaces. She considered mulching with peat and sawdust, tried it and decided it compounded her problems. A wild

garden was not what she wanted; she began considering how closely she could plant two or three species together to achieve maximum use of space and minimum growth of weeds. She studied once more the Jekyll plantings in *Garden Colour* and frequently repeated her phrase 'Miss Jekyll was right, as usual', deciding that if Bowles could accommodate such a wide range of species, that might be the best course for her, too, and thus help to eliminate the tiresome work of weeding. Her main borders were accordingly planted in a skilled manner and she evolved what became the Margery Fish style.

Her plants were selected according to three main criteria: the colours of the developing foliage, flowers and seed heads; the plant's ability to grow happily with neighbouring species without smothering them; and the tolerance of the plant to the conditions in which it was expected to grow. Her success in exploiting these factors is undisputed. She referred to her method privately as slum gardening and it required constant attention to keep alive the entity. In essence it worked, and gave pleasure and inspiration to thousands who copied her style.

A piece from *The Garden Notebook* of Constance Spry (1940) was probably the inspiration of Margery's ideas on the placing of individual plants to give the effect of a living tapestry of colour. At that time they were not followed in many gardens.

> The beauty of a border lies not only in the colour grouping but also in the clever juxtaposition of contrasting shapes. Plants of one type, habit, and form of foliage look well set next to strongly contrasting forms; a vigorous leaf by a filmy one, a slender spire by a massive head. This contributes to the general effect. An instance of this would be the planting of the grey mullein *(Verbascum broussa)* with its fine grey leaves and thickly white-felted stem, next to the filmy cloud of *Gypsophila paniculata*, of the airy flowers of the yellow *Isatis glauca* beside the spires of yellow lupin.

GARDENING FRIENDS

Life in Somerset during the war tended to be insular, and Margery became a close friend of two very experienced gardeners nearby.

Brympton d'Evercy, near Yeovil, was one of the greatest of the houses along the A30, its garden well established when Vita Sackville-West was

a frequent visitor. It is illustrated in a book of 1892, *The Formal Garden in England*, by Reginald Blomfield and Inigo Thomas, and in Inigo Triggs' great book *Formal Gardens*, published by private subscription in 1902.

Its owner, Mrs Clive Ponsonby Fane, had for some time experimented with different aspects of the style of gardening Margery eventually adopted. Her garden too included sun, shade, moisture, trees and walls. Though an amateur, who probably discussed the aims of her gardening only with others directly involved, Mrs Clive too had been growing uncommon hedgerow plants and cottage flowers, like the now-famous Brympton Red pink: Lady Lilian Digby of Lewcombe, Evershot, Dorset, had seen this flowering at the workhouse in Beaminster one day when visiting, and all the plants sold today derive from the slip she took. Her plantings of crimson and silver by the lake at Brympton created a long period of colour which Margery always enjoyed. Although the family house in Ireland had been sold by the time Margery was acquainted, Mrs Clive gave her the entry to many Irish gardens which Margery scoured for lost plants.

The second friend who discussed gardening in some depth with her was Phyllis Reiss. Her garden at Tintinhull tended to be overshadowed by the proximity of the strongly architectural features of Montacute, two miles away, so Mrs Reiss emphasised the 'green stonework' of well-planted and trimmed topiary, as a background for the strong colours of herbaceous perennials. These three ladies rarely altered their gardens without discussing it with each other.

As Margery became more and more popular for her writing and gardening she gathered around her many young people, who either had established gardens of their own or had embarked upon a career in horticulture. Margery gave them the benefit of her experience and plants. Among these friends were many now well-known gardeners, such as Christopher Brickell, the present secretary of the Royal Horticultural Society, Penelope Hobhouse, now custodian of Tintinhull, Christopher Lloyd, Valerie Finnis, Fred Whitsey, Joyce Heathcoat Amory, Netta Statham and Tony Venison, all of whom readily acknowledge the pleasure the acquaintanceship gave them.

5

Cottage Gardening

The words cottage gardening have different meanings for different people. Sometimes the white garden at Sissinghurst is described as 'cottagey' or the use of a single colour in a garden is called a 'cottage-garden effect'. Frequently claims are made that Margery Fish was the mother of English cottage gardening, but for almost 150 years previously the cottage *orné* had been a feature of the countryside, reaching its pinnacle in the Edwardian cottage garden depicted by the watercolours of Helen Allingham.

The Hon Mrs Ewing wrote a charming Edwardian children's story called 'Mary's Meadow'. It told of a child who found some hose-in-hose cowslips as illustrated in Parkinson, and created her own garden of these flowers. Mrs Emerson, of The Leeke, Limavady, in Ireland, unashamedly based the plant descriptions in her catalogue on this story, and Margery equally tended towards this aspect of her cottage garden. But she could still not stop experimenting with a single-coloured garden.

Although Margery grew many species and varieties of plants, frequently well over 2,000 cultivars, she has become best known for growing the flowers of English cottage gardens. She loved these plants and when she wrote about them she wrote from the heart. 'Plants are friendly creatures and enjoy each other's company. The close-packed plants in a cottage garden grow well and look happy', she claimed. Also, one of her great pleasures was to take a walk in the country and gather wild flowers. As she widened the scope of her gardening, she found that many of these plants would merge into the background when out of flower, and could be used to further her ideas of having a flower in bloom ever day of the year.

'No definite design went into their planting, and the treasured flowers were put wherever there was room.' These cottage-garden flowers were the first she saw blooming in her neighbours' gardens when she

began to take an interest in gardening. Because they cannot be grouped botanically, they are more easily considered individually.

PRIMROSES

'No other flower seems quite so much at home in the cottage garden as does the Primrose', she wrote in *Cottage Garden Flowers* (1961). The wild primroses in the hedgerows around East Lambrook increased Margery's interest. She would frequently list 100 different cultivars in her nursery list, but was always recalling how she had gone through a vase of fifty cultivars, and chosen a wild one as the best for its clear colour. She was especially fond of the cultivars that were illustrated in the herbals of Gerard and Parkinson, particularly the double primrose and polyanthus called hose-in-hose – named from the Elizabethan-style hose, one coming out of the other, as one flower comes out of the other. These can be reproduced from seed. Margery mixed the yellow and orange shades in small borders and added a hose-in-hose cowslip given her by Miss Wynne of Avoca.

Another primrose form which can be grown from seed is the Jack-in-the-green, where each flower is surrounded by a small ruff of green leaves. Margery's special preference was for the double primroses; as Gerard said in 1588, 'No Sweeter, nor prettier flower ever warmed to bloom under a northern sun'.

Double primroses in her day were not be grown from seed, and some of the old varieties, of which at one time she had thirty, were becoming diseased. During the hot summer of 1959 many varieties started to weaken, but some are still in commerce today. Among these are Alba Plena (double white), Quaker's Bonnet (double lilac), Our Pat (double *juliae* Wanda), a double pink *juliae*, as well as Bon Accord Gem, rose-lilac, and her personal favourite Red Paddy. This is a crimson flower with a white edging; of great beauty, it remains a good grower. Margery loved her double primroses like children, giving them her best compost and finest positions, though they behaved as capriciously for her as for everyone else. She grew many hundreds of primrose seedlings annually and after a few years selected for her nursery her finest colours: Lambrook Mauve, Peach and Yellow are still grown today, some thirty years after they were first distributed.

FLORISTS' FLOWERS

With polyanthus she broke new ground. For 150 years what were loosely termed florists' (ie fanciers') flowers in the early 1800s had not been fashionable in the gardens of the middle class and aristocracy. By growing the gold and silver laced polyanthus she made a whole generation take notice, grow auriculas, pinks and carnations and look again at the form of their hyacinths and roses. (Sadly her soil would not grow good tulips, the most exotic of all the florist flowers, so she was unable to show people their uses in a garden). She grew show auriculas in some quantity, and also a multitude of the older border types, such as Old Irish Blue, Crimson Black, Blue Velvet and the Red and Yellow Dusty Millers. She never really mastered how to grow them well; though she tried almost every situation possible, she never came to terms with the fact that in the high winter rainfall and mostly mild temperatures of Somerset auriculas needed better winter drainage than she could provide.

PINKS

Her large collections of pinks were used in and on her walls – the fine old laced pinks in raised beds, to help them resist wet, wintry conditions. She had a remarkable eye for a good plant and her Double Dark Red clove carnation is a good plant still; she will be remembered for publicising the pink Brympton Red. The old laced pinks again were 'florists' flowers' of the type condemned by Miss Jekyll and William Robinson as artificial. With their black edging on a white ground they were highly decorative edging plants and could be used for foliage effect throughout the year.

DAISIES AND DOUBLE FLOWERS

Another species she assiduously collected, and not only as ground cover for the roses, was the daisy. 'No self-respecting cottage garden would be without its little edging of daisies', she wrote in 1961 (*Cottage*

Garden Flowers). From her first days in the garden when she planted Dresden China daisies in the paving gaps, she enjoyed them. Most of the old Victorian daisies had by this time disappeared, but she grew pink Mavoureen, red Rob Roy and white Robert. A small daisy from Ireland with narrow crimson petals and a large centre she distributed among her growing number of cottage-plant enthusiasts. Her secret joy whenever depressed, if the weather was acceptable, was to split up her 'hen-and-chickens daisy'. This plant, 'Jackanapes-on-horseback', with its habit of producing a double daisy surrounded by flowers of small single daisies, had been grown since Elizabethan times. It was one of her standby plants to grow in damp rich soil with a little shade. 'Double flowers have always been popular with cottage gardeners' *(Cottage Garden Flowers)*. For more rigorous conditions the stronger-growing Alba Plena, of Sacheverell Sitwell's *Old Fashioned Flowers*, was mixed with the golden-leaved single daisy. 'For some reason double flowers seem to go with old gardens; they have a quaintness and a something that goes with sun bonnets and print frocks.'

Margery's interest in saving older cottage-garden flowers helped her· pursue her love of double flowers – cottage flowers meaning attractive wild flowers or forms of attractive wild flowers that differ from the type. Her conversations with E.A. Bowles on what he called his 'lunatic asylum' of unusual old forms encouraged her to widen her horizons to representatives of the first Elizabethan garden plants. She rediscovered the double red wallflower Old Bloody Warrior, although when propagating it she reversed the adjectives. She grew the double yellow Harpur Crewe, and another pale yellow scented one. This mingled well with her double sweet rocket, another plant of Stuart gardens difficult to keep going because it needs early spring propagation. The double mauve *Cardamine pratensis* (lady's smock or cuckoo flower) was another favourite for the ditch garden, although some of its seedlings came single.

The white bachelor's buttons, or fair maids of France, *Ranunculus aconitifolius* Flore Pleno, had great personality despite its slow increase, and became a May-flowering standby. More brilliant was the double *Lychnis viscaria* Flore Pleno, which needs regular division, flowering in company with double buttercups, like *Ranunculus bulbosus* Flore Pleno, or *R.acris* Flore Pleno. Their golden colours complemented the bright carmine of the *Lychis*.

'Pudding Trees'. The Cupressus path of clipped *Cupressus lawsoniana Fletcheri* created a foil for the plants of earlier centuries

The small white *Saxifraga granulata* Flore Pleno with its neat brown roots was probably the plant referred to as 'pretty maids all in a row' in the nursery rhyme; the 'silver bells' were possibly the double-flowered white form of *Campanula trachelium*, which is probably the true Canterbury bell, but is also called Coventry bell. The double-flowered *Geranium pratense* with its shades of silver to dark blue is again a wild flower brought to the garden. Margery grew double-flowering hollyhocks as much for their charm as the fact that they flowered during her August gap.

Double violets like *Viola odorata* Duchesse de Parme in lavender, Marie Louise in darker blue, and Comte de Brazza in white, needed some winter protection for their flowers, but they, with the dwarf double dark crimson sweet William, were the essence of East Lambrook planting, as was the double marsh marigold in the ditch garden. Margery continued to seek but never grew the double cyclamen and double martagon lily, first recorded in 1676 and rediscovered by George Morison Taylor in a West Lothian garden during the late 1940s. This remains rare to this day.

Herbs piled on plants in such close friendliness she could not hope to get between to weed. Antirrhinum, aquilegia and astrantia grew on

top of each other. Astrantias, the old English Hattie's pincushion or melancholy gentleman, fitted Margery's idea of cottage plants and did well at East Lambrook. Numerous variations occurred in the seedlings and one which caught her eye she named 'Shaggy'; later on it was widely sold in the nursery trade as 'Margery Fish'. Bergamot too suited the garden; large clumps grew with different mints, with costmary (*Chrysanthemum balsamita balsamitoides*) and southernwood or lad's love, *Artemesia abrotanum*. She grew wormwood, *Artemesia absinthium*, from seed regularly and Lambrook Silver was a fine form she selected for the nursery.

BULBS

Bulbs at East Lambrook were difficult, other than narcissi. Much of the soil was not sufficiently well drained for them to grow as well as Walter had trained Margery to desire. Tulips, for example, would be planted in a clump and almost dared to survive. Hyacinths were not widely used outside bowls. However, crown imperial (*Fritillaria imperialis*) was planted and enjoyed every spring. This native of northern Persia and Afghanistan was given pride of place by Parkinson in his great gardening book of 1612, but by the time Margery saw it in a few cottage gardens it had fallen from favour. Mrs Earle records in 1900 in *Pot Pourri from a Surrey Garden* that it was always considered 'cottagey' and better ignored, but she enjoyed it, and grew it widely. In the fenlands of northern Cambridgeshire it had the conditions it revelled in, an alkaline peat with good drainage. During the Second World War, early experiments were made with skin grafts using a paste of the bulbs, and so even here they had become unusual. Margery mixed the orange and yellow together, the only varieties she could find, although George Morison Taylor had recorded eight in his *Old Fashioned Flowers* in 1946, a generation before Margery gardened.

'The daffodils that grew in the old gardens are not those we usually buy today', she wrote in *Cottage Garden Flowers*. She rarely added a new variety of daffodil; Beersheba was the creamy-white she enjoyed, but she found great pleasure in collecting old double-flowering forms. *Narcissus capax plenus*, Queen Anne's double daffodil, was her preference, and she added *minor* Flore Pleno, Rip Van Winkle, single Queen

The hedge of angelica, which separated the herb garden from the lawn, was a typical use of native plants for a decorative effect

of Spain and the old Van Sion known by Parkinson. The soil at East Lambrook suited most daffodils, and she distributed the rarer ones she discovered on her lecture tours; bulbs from many of these have been returned to East Lambrook now the garden is being restored.

MARGERY'S PERSONAL PREFERENCES

If asked which of these old English plants she enjoyed most, she would probably have said primroses, and generally not the most difficult plants: pulmonarias, for their early spring colour; and the host of double flowers she collected – double buttercup *(Ranunculus acris* Flore Pleno); and fair maids of France *(Ranunculus aconitifolius* Flore Pleno); the double lychnis, and the aquilegias before they were improved; the double marsh marigold, and the double meadow saxifrage – these seemed to her the essence of the type of cottage-garden plant she was endeavouring to conserve for another generation. She did this so successfully, that today, some thirty years later, her name is remembered for the warmth and encouragement she gave to the thousands of people

who adapted her style to their own gardens, and extended their range of plantings by following her example.

THE GREEN GARDEN

As the garden at East Lambrook developed, so small areas had to be replanned to accommodate the extra plants. An area near the barton, no more than 50ft square, standing some 6 or 7 ft higher than the entrance drive, needed an added interest. She had recently completed her silver garden (discussed in Chapter 7), on a south-facing slope on the other side of the garden, and decided that this was to be her area for green flowers.

Eleanour Sinclair Rohde had written at some length about early spring and green turning into gold in *Gardens of Delight* in 1934, and discussed her delight in the green foliaceous primrose; the book had influenced Margery in her early days of gardening and may have done so here. However, 1950 was the era of Constance Spry and Women's Insititute enthusiasm for flower arranging. Like all lecturers on a theme, Constance Spry needed new thoughts to interest her audiences, and maintain the sales of her books. On one of her visits to East Lambrook she saw the flowers of the green primrose, at a time when she was working green flowers into her arrangements. For both ladies the idea of green flowers was a stimulus; Constance Spry saw the green in some of Margery's hellebores, and reworked the idea of using molucella, or bells of Ireland, into her arrangements. It must have been flattering to Margery that one of the personalities of the time should come for advice on plants, and may well have helped her decide on a green-flowered garden. It was of its nature small and special; the site was not really suitable for the green primrose, but Margery planted these beneath a hazel, a good combination. Another plant was the green rose, *Rosa chinensis viridiflora*, more curious than beautiful, with its green and crimson inflorescence. *Fritillaria pyrenaica* with its olive-green flowers filled a space to be taken over by the annual Bells of Ireland. Margery never found the completely green 'Lenten rose' she sought, but each year her seedling hellebores became a shade nearer it; and her wood anemone with green and blue bracts was compensation.

At the risk of attributing too much influence to Eleanour Sinclair

Rohde's *Gardens of Delight*, her remarks there that green flowers seem to have been much admired in the seventeenth century were certainly relevant to the type of green garden Margery was creating at East Lambrook. Looking at its layout today, it takes the pattern of a seventeenth-century parterre garden.

Most green-flowered plants suitable for flower arrangers, such as hellebores, *Garrya elliptica* and the greener snowdrops, bloom early in the year. Some prefer to grow in shade, such as Solomon's seal and *Hacquetia epipactis (Dondia epipactis)* or need a subdued light for their quiet, cool beauty; their late summer rival is the green hyacinth, *Galtonia princeps*. Margery grasped these ideas quickly and added some of the easier green-flowered hardy orchids such as the man orchid *Aceras anthropophorum*, but perhaps the plant which most completely fulfilled her ideas was the great rose plantain, *Plantago major rosularis*. This plant was known and loved by Elizabethan gardeners; Parkinson commented that 'Instead of the long slender spike or ears that the ordinary plantain hath a number of such small green leaves lay'd roundwise like unto the same roote'.

Annuals For Character

To extend the colour and interest of the green area later in the season, she used a large number of annuals, sown at the end of April and early May. These were also planted elsewhere in the garden. Margery had never been adverse to growing annuals: in her first year at East Lambrook she had planted them to make a quick show of colour, and remarked that it was the only time she ever achieved flowers like the pictures on the packets! Some fifteen years further into gardening she became extremely selective in those she planted. Cornflowers, snapdragons, scabious and marigold were obviously at home, as were biennials such as foxgloves, sweet williams and Canterbury bells. Margery added a further dimension by discovering a hen-and-chicken marigold. She realised how ephemeral were the poppies and other annuals of the cottage gardens she loved, as she walked or drove through Somerset. Growing annual flowers must be time-consuming and the planting, saving seed and storing were tasks Margery saved mostly for herself, even though there were times when the entire nursery took on the aspect of an Elizabethan stillroom.

6

Ground-cover Plants

'From the aesthetic angle I think most gardeners agree that a garden well clothed is more attractive than one with vast expanses of bare soil, and added beauty by contrast or harmony can be achieved by the use of plants of different colour or form, Margery commented in her book *Ground Cover Plants*. Of the three friends who interchanged ideas, Margery Fish, Phyllis Reiss and Mrs Clive Ponsonby Fane, the latter had the most original interest in ground-cover plants. Her attempt to cover an area in crimson and silver on the far side of the lake at Brympton encouraged Margery to use leaf-colour in her quest for colour in the garden every day of the year. She extended her search for plants of good leaf form and colouring that would give a period of flower and then still provide an attractive background ground-cover for succeeding flowers; and if the plant was not too invasive but a good grower, it would even block out the weeds. The differing terrains of her garden allowed experiments with plants in varying situations.

The first lesson learned was the importance of keeping the soil in good condition – hence her emphasis on making and using compost. Her book *Ground Cover Plants* shows how seriously she took the subject, and the extent to which she experimented with the use of leaves for striking effect. Although the great garden of Hestercombe was in decline, the bergenias Miss Jekyll had used there as edging had survived, and Margery frequently used bergenias or heucheras as effective edgings.

TYPICAL GROUND COVER-PLANTING

A delightful combination was to use the fernlike leaves of *Geranium atlanticum* as a background for colchicums. This bulbous geranium from the Atlas Mountains made low 6in leaves in autumn, among the flowers of the autumn crocus; in spring the position reversed, the bright blue flowers among the straplike Colchicum foliage giving welcome colour for long periods in damp shade under trees. Margery's use of pulmonarias

Thick planting of different species eliminated the need for weeding on the terraces

was then rarely seen – in masses of varying colours, using the spotted leaves as a feature until they flowered in the spring.

She was inspired to use sweet Cicely by a visit to Anne Hathaway's cottage at Stratford-on-Avon, enjoying the tracery of the leaves in contrast to fatsia and mahonia. Some plants had to be rejected as ground cover because they were too neat; others like *Nepeta faassenii* and *Phuopsis stylosa*, with its bright pink flowers, would smother weeds throughout the season. She used the broad leathery leaves of *Limonium latifolium* to cover the ground and fill the space between shrubs and tall herbaceous perennials with its flowers. When the shrubs were taller she used *Pimpinella major*, the pink cow-parsley, with its good foliage and dull pink flowers.

Where the garden was hot and dry, santolinas were planted for height, or as a dwarf contrast the silver-grey leaves of *Dorycnium hirsutum*. Another plant that enjoys hot dry sunshine is helianthemum and these mixed their colours with *Erigeron mucronatus* and *Gypsophila repens*.

The lady's mantle, *Alchemilla mollis*, with its greeny-yellow flowers and round, widely pleated leaves, associated well with *Geranium*

wallichianum Buxton's Blue, smothering any weeds around. So did the salmon-pink *Geranium endressii*, which she grew between her 'pudding trees' (*Chamaecyparis lawsoniana* Fletcheri), and Eleagnus. The hardy fuchsias Mrs Popple and Tom Thumb were excellent smother shrubs, but by nature more suited to the herbaceous border for autumn colour; they did not give all-year cover as satisfactorily as *Euphorbia robbiae*.

Foxgloves were good in their growth style, but symphytums were too strong for effective use in the herbaceous border: sometimes she allowed some variegated forms to flourish, but they were never satisfactory for her purposes. Two other plants she discarded were *Trachystemon orientale* and *Brunnera macrophylla*, both of which grew too coarse in the increasingly fertile conditions as she mulched her garden annually. *Phlomis viscosa*, with flat rosettes of large leaves, would reliably cover the ground left vacant by early-flowering companions. It was rarely deadheaded, its late flowers being left to furnish the winter borders.

Hardy geraniums were reliable ground cover. *Ibericum*, with dark leaves, looked best in a border, but Margery was particularly pleased with *G. platypetalum* underneath *Magnolia grandiflora* Exmouth. The geranium's close root system did not allow weeds to penetrate to spoil the planting, an asset also offered by geraniums *reflexum* and *punctatum*, with their changing leaves bringing interesting colours beyond their flowering period. The grey-green leaves of *Geranium renardii* against a red-leaved shrub were good, but her personal choice was as a foil for silver leaves. It is surprising that, though she grew four cultivars of *Geranium macrorrhizum*, with its dwarf habit and aromatic leaves, she rarely used it as a carpeting plant for taller plants to grow through.

The silvery-green leaves of *Centaurea dealbata* (perennial cornflower) produced large mounds nearly 2ft tall, as well as pink flowers, and they became almost as good fillers of space as the blue *Centaurea montana*. Doronicums were an effective foil in spring with their succession of yellow daisy flowers. She preferred the taller old variety Harpur Crewe, planting it in close association with *Polemonium* Lambrook Mauve. All the polemoniums have good neat foliage, reproduce well from both seed and offsets, and with their country name of Jacob's ladder felt right for the garden. Lambrook Mauve was a good colour variation from the type, which ranges from white to pale blue and pink.

Margery Fish

50

Herbaceous ground cover in poor soil in the sun is difficult. *Erodium manescavi*, with its white stars, grew from June to the first frost; it was more reliably perennial and better colour than *Anthemis tinctoria* Grallagh Gold. White *Lysimachia clethroides* was usually able to tolerate drier conditions than the coarser *Lysimachia punctata* (yellow loose-strife). These strong-growing plants were occasionally blended with a dragon's head, *Dracocephalum prattii*. *Nepeta macrantha* was a good shade of blue. Blue was also supplied by *Amsonia salicifolia*, but for shade she generally preferred the less invasive thalictrums. In borders where moist shade could be left to itself she planted bulbs, ferns and the old double day-lily *Hemerocallis fulva* Flore Pleno.

TIDY GROUND COVER FOR DEEP SHADE

The deep soil under trees could be a difficult gardening proposition if left to become overgrown or swamped with weeds. She considered creeping Jenny, *Lysimachia nummularia*, one of the best plants for ground cover here, preferring the golden form. It grew round the stones at the bottom of the ditch garden, with *Mitella breweri* used as a contrasting green shade to the banks with double primroses, trilliums and the arum family. By working its way over the soil with its tidy flat leaves the mitella made a thick ground cover. She would inspect the small sprays of green flowers with a magnifying glass!

Woodland conditions of mixed sun and shade suited a wide range of plants, but where the area was densely shaded she used barrenworts (epimediums). Their congested roots stopped weeds growing through, and the leaves had good colour and a tight form. Another green flower was *Rubus fockeanus*, with its prostrate rooting and crinkled green leaves; but this was one for a peaty soil and Margery never had enough to try it on lime. In contrast mother-of-thousands (*Saxifraga stolonifera*) spread quickly: it is not generally considered hardy but proved so at East Lambrook.

Papaver orientalis (oriental poppies)

By the Malthouse, with eucalyptus, fuchsias, euphorbias and clematis

A visit to A.T. Johnson's plantsman's garden in the Conway Valley made her realise the value of *Arum proboscideum* in damp shade. She saw these plants carpeting large areas, looking like small mice and realised how fascinating its flowers could be in spring. The scent of the native woodruff *Asperula odorata* is effective on a shady slope and the foliage effect of baneberries good for most of the year – she used *Actaea rubra* with its red berries after spikes of white flowers, as well as *Actaea spicata*, the rare native with black berries, a good companion for the white alternative form *Actaea spicata* Alba.

The whole family of polygonatum or Solomon's seal were excellent for blocking weed growth under moist trees. The thick-rooted variety *multiflorum* was a strong-growing plant, and with her determination to extend the range of her cultivars she added *Polygonatum officinale*, and its rare double-flowering form. Various forms of lily-of-the-valley, *Convallaria majalis*, were grown at East Lambrook. The golden-variegated and double-flowering were too precious to be left to rough it, but under walls or round trees she enjoyed both scent and colour of the pink and white forms mixed together. *Liriope graminifolia* is often used as a lawn or an edging in Italy. In England it is usually planted in association with nerines, because their flowering periods complement each other. Margery's best plants grew in moist woodland, and she abandoned hope of adding in nerines.

With hostas once again she showed her gardening skill, and where she led thousands followed. In shade and by the waterside they were planted as contrast to *Iris sibirica*. *Hosta crispula*, Thomas Hogg and *albomarginata* with their white markings showed up well in dark places, but did not cover as much space as *H. undulata* and *fortunei*. For large leaves her choice was *Hosta ventricosa* with its dark violet flowers, or the smaller heart-shaped leaves of *sieboldiana*. She experimented with some fifty different forms of hostas, liking their attractive tidy leaves and stately flowers. They were more satisfactory ground cover than plants like tiarella or astrantia, *Physalis franchetti*, or the Japanese anemones which tended to grow too coarsely for her taste. This did not stop her using carefully some of the larger easily grown plants like *Spiraea aruncus (Aruncus sylvester)*, teasels and particularly the soft lavender *Lactuca bourgaei* with its excellent leaf form but bad habit of self-seeding: like the cottage peonies, these were a little too easy to grow to stimulate her interest in the way that double primroses did.

CARPETING PLANTS

The constant searching for a suitable background for primroses led to experiments with carpeting plants. She never found a perfect foil for primroses, but found many excellent ways of using small plants as she experimented.

The first surprise was the success of creeping thymes in the shade. *Thymus serpyllum* is usually grown in full sun, but in shade it made a solid mat of aromatic foliage about a foot square, which during July was covered with flowers, ranging in colour from white to crimson; *Thymus serpyllum coccineus* was the deepest, then Pink Chintz, followed by the white Albus, usually the last to flower. Two other thymes grown were dwarf *hirsutus doerfleri*, and *herba-barona* from Corsica, so named because its strong caraway scent and flavour were used in cooking barons of beef.

Another plant with useful aromatic foliage was pennyroyal, *Mentha pulegium*. The creeping form was good for carpeting, and she preferred it before the pinkish flowers arrived; with it she planted pointed-leaved *Mentha gattefossei*. The tiny *Mentha requienii*, also Corsican, had delightful small leaves but persistently invaded the lawn.

Mossy saxifrages did well at East Lambrook, covering the soil and growing better in shade than sun. A pale pink called Apple Blossom, which Margery bought on arrival, grew between paving stones in the front garden, and its fast increase made it a useful border for flower beds. Phyllis Reiss used it at Tintinhull to border a long bed of shades of blue iris: Margery felt this was one of the best effects there and frequently commented on it in her lectures. Other varieties of saxifrages she grew included James Brenner, with its large white flowers on 6in stalks, contrasted with Elf and Dwarf in pale pink. Sir David Haig, deep crimson, complemented the deep salmon-pink of Mrs Piper, with Margery's personal preference, the deep pink Dartington Double. Most of her gardening life she experimented with a carpet of mossy saxifrages. She concluded the best one was *Saxifraga hypnoides* gemmifera with white flowers and foliage which turned crimson in the autumn; it hugged the ground like a mat and eliminated weeds.

If the mossy saxifrages had a wider colour range, she would have

found the perfect carpeting plant. The rock phloxes had more colours, but they really needed good drainage and sunny conditions. She grew alpine phlox in between autumn shrubs to carry colour through the season in the garden and among the varieties of *Phlox subulata* (mossy phlox) were soft lavender G.F. Wilson, Pink Betty, Sprite with a carmine eye, Samson and Model in varying shades of pink. The variety Temiscaming was planted separately because of its violet cerise colour. *Phlox douglasii* is neater, with mats about 1ft square against the 2ft of *subulata*. The best was lavender Boothman's Variety, mauve with a violet centre. May Snow had white flowers, *rosea* was a flat silvery pink, complemented by Eva, Gem and Violet Queen in shades of lavender and purple.

One or two of the veronicas were used as carpeters. In sun and shade *Veronica peduncularis* Rosea, pink and white on the outside and deep rose within, flowered in May and June. Two low-growing shrubs were also used: *Veronica fruticans* behaved like a herbaceous plant with small dark leaves on prostrate stems and bright blue flowers in April and May; and a relative of the ground-cover St John's wort, *Hypericum reptans* had fresh evergreen foliage, with flat golden flowers from July to September.

Two small but invasive plants Margery planted in paths were *Cotula squalida* and *Cotula pyrethrifolia*. Acaenas took precedence in situations where their invasiveness was not important, principally *Acaena buchananii, glaucophylla, sanguisorbae, microphylla* and the bronze-leaved, purple-flowered *Acaena novae-zealandiae. Antennaria dioica* Rosea never grew higher than 2in with pale pink fluffy flowers; *tomentosa* in creamy-white and Rubra in rosy-red grew to 3in, and these plants were used as ground cover for some of the smaller fritillaries such as *meleagris*, in which Margery, Mrs Clive, Phyllis Reiss, and Vita Sackville-West all had a particular interest.

A range of neat-growing alpine plants was used to create suitable low cover for the front of the border. Among these were *Helichrysum bellidiodes, Frankenia laevis* and *thymifolia, Mazus reptans* and *Herniaria glabra*.

Not so successful in carpeting were the dwarf creeping Jenny

View along the ditch. *Lamium maculatum* covered the ground and accentuated the spikes of euphorbia and iris in the ditch garden

Looking east in the front garden. Low ground cover softened the paving and accentuated the roses on the walls

(Lysimachia japonica minutissima) or the 'Corsican curse', *Helxine soleirolii*: these invasive plants carpeted so well Margery wished she had never seen them. Some of the plants which ramped away beyond control were good, others simply a pervasive nuisance. One of the best plants to cover ground quickly was the alpine strawberry; in the collection were the Plymouth strawberry and the darker-leafed *Fragaria indica*, the variegated-leaved woodland strawberry, as well as the double-flowering variety.

Her original use of lamiums did much to popularise the species. *Lamium galeobdolon* Variegatum in particular was useful for softening paths and walls; and once growing too quickly it was easily dismantled in contrast to *Cerastium tomentosum* (snow-in-summer) with its invasive roots and ability to grow wherever the soil is dry and poor. If this beautiful plant could be controlled, it would be one of the best silver-leafed carpeters available.

Another plant with good contrasting foliage was the bugle, *Ajuga reptans*. With their blue flowers, the red-leaved and rainbow-leaved variegated forms were a welcome contrast in the garden despite their

invasiveness. *Sedum spurium* was a vigorous plant which covered rough areas; Margery used the pink flowers in contrast to the white Album, and the blood-red Schorbusser Blut. She considered *Campanula poscharskyana* an ally, with its bright green foliage and long period of lavender-coloured bells in the summer, but the white form too weak for effective colour. Campanulas used as ground cover were *C.portenschlagiana* (or *muralis*), and *C.garganica* with its starry, light blue flowers. For shade she felt that the Jerusalem violet, *Campanula glomerata*, with its bright flowers and rustic charm, was particularly right for East Lambrook. The final ramper was *Campanula latiloba*, which she found welcome in such difficult places as under holly bushes: here, in competition with *Vinca acutiloba* and *V.major*, a good weed-free cover could be maintained. These periwinkles were far too good to be ignored. The variegated-leaved *major* grew obligingly between dark shrubs like *Cotoneaster horizontalis*, or down banks under trees.

Coloured Carpet for the Terraced Garden

Margery discussed with a more experienced gardening cousin her idea of a tapestry of dwarf plants of different coloured leaves on her terraced garden, using the dark green of *Iberis sempervirens* as a background. Unusually for her she did not carry all the arguments, and had to concede that having too much of the same plant did not work well in a garden. Very gradually as she extended her knowledge she planted more varieties of *Iberis sempervirens* for a change of height, and looked around for alternative plants to extend the evergreen planting. She used *Waldsteinia ternata* with its yellow flowers in spring for its ability to cope with dry shade, and and a visit to Hardwick Hall convinced her of the benefit of London pride *(Saxifraga umbrosa)* in a wide border for both sun and shade.

The evergreen geums, such as *montanum* or *rivale*, were not tough enough to give a good account of themselves in dry shade. The long-branching potentillas, like Roxana, Gibson's Scarlet and Miss Willmott were not tidy enough; she preferred *potentilla x tonguei* here, and relegated *Potentilla montana* to work merely as a trailing plant.

The most satisfactory answer to carpeting here, she concluded,

was to use violets; she was among the best violet growers this country has known, supplying Hillier's nurseries as well as her own for many years. Violets provided evergreen cover when she needed it and over her gardening life she found they would grow in both sun and shade – she graded them accordingly, with the small *Viola sulphurea* growing alongside the bright blue John Raddenbury, and giving the pink Coeur d'Alsace a south-facing position. The larger coarser foliage of the luxuriant *Viola* the Czar made a focal point with its white flowers contrasting with the red-purple L'Arne, the softer blue-grey of French Grey contrasting with the red-violet of Admiral Avellan. These she found were the best ground coverers – larger-flowered varieties such as Governor Herrick or Princess of Wales did not make such firm mats nor seed as freely. Even Margery never achieved early flowering of double and semi-double violets without the use of cloches or frames. After her death, interest in violets waned, and many of hers became extremely rare.

A successful ground-cover plant was *Omphalodes cappadocica* (blue-eyed Mary); the flowers of forget-me-not blue lasted well and the plant spread, but only tidily. Similarly, *Myosotis dissitiflora* a perennial self-seeding forget-me-not, had good evergreen leaves but no popular name. Myosotis leaves are a slightly lighter colour and rather glossier than the ordinary forget-me-not; they were used to make ground cover between trees in her mixed borders.

A plant which Margery felt she should use more frequently in this situation was *Campanula persicifolia*, with its blue and white spires of cup-shaped flowers, grown in our gardens since the time of Parkinson. She preferred the cup-and-saucer type, but found neither they nor the rarer, beautiful double forms had long lives. The reason was that the double-flowering ones need transplanting in early spring, like the double sweet rocket *Hesperis matronalis* Flore Pleno, a plant Margery liked, but was unable to grow successfully. Her difficulties with campanulas encouraged use of the more common arabis, aubretia and erigeron in low-growing, almost carpeting, situations. For years Margery had grown the low fleshy *Erigeron glaucus*, but found it too unruly for neater conditions, whereas both forms of *Arabis albida* made attractive shaggy ground-cover; she vastly preferred the double form,

The terraces were always green with plants growing rapidly with ample moisture from the paving

The path to the privy became a successful experiment in creating a living tapestry, using *Skimmia japonica* and *Chamaecyparis lawsoniana Fletcheri* as ground work

although the single was useful for rough places. Aubretias would soon cover the ground if planted a foot apart and stayed green all year if clipped tight after flowering.

The pale pink flowers, veined with crimson, of *Geranium sanguineum lancastriense*, one of her improved forms of the native bloody cranesbill, appealed to her because of its long flowering period and the crimson and gold tints of the leaves in autumn. *Stachys macrantha* Superba did not make such a close clump but its deeply veined leaves made a pleasant contrast to gold and silver leaves. It was used for ground cover for the rose Frau Dagmar Hastrup, the two soft pink flowers blending together most successfully.

For neat evergreen ground cover, probably epimediums were the favourite plants for both Margery and Phyllis Reiss. Phyllis Reiss cut off all the leaves in early spring so only the flowers made a show in the broad bands of *Epimedium pinnatum colchicum* that bordered the

courtyard beds near the house at Tintinhull. *Epimedium perralderianum* was also good twelve-month cover with its yellow flowers and glossy toothed leaves which turn crimson and chestnut in autumn. Prunella or self-heal is another neat-growing carpet plant for ground cover if regularly dead-headed and top-dressed, as it exhausts the soil it grows in. *Grandiflora* in violet is the largest, while blue, pink and white forms are almost always available.

Wherever possible in all this round-the-year foliage ground-cover, the smaller polyanthus were planted, such as Kinlough Beauty, The Bride or creamy-yellow dwarf Lady Greer admired by the Queen Mother at the RHS Show in March 1952, and the double-flowering Old Rose. Sometimes the purple foliage of the Garryarde polyanthus was planted as a contrast, interspersed among *Gentiana acaulis*, which with its tight ground-hugging growth gave an added bonus if it could be persuaded to flower.

These plants, for which careful good gardening was needed, were in complete contrast to the hearty *Polygonum affine* which Margery admired at Killerton, near Exeter, where it still carpeted a hillside after almost a century of neglect. From August to October the soft pink flowers pleased her immensely, but she never let the polygonums ramp away too wildly at East Lambrook despite her delight in the rich brown leaves in the winter.

ROSES FOR GROUND COVER – OR GROUND COVER FOR ROSES

Margery confessed to ambiguity over roses. She did not like too many in the garden, though her friends at Tintinhull, Brympton d'Evercy and Sissinghurst were all using the older roses for colour effect during June and sometimes as ground cover during the rest of the season. But though she did not lecture frequently on roses for ground cover, or ground cover for roses – and when she did was less convincing than on many other subjects – she made some attempt to bring roses into her planting scheme.

One way in which she used hybrid perpetual roses was to peg down their long trails. Frau Karl Druschki (Snowqueen) is one white which is better grown like this because the lack of scent is less disappointing

The paved terrace walk and the stone seat were further examples of skilful use of texture, colour and form

with the flowers at ground level. Mrs John Laing was a favourite pink rose, but flowers so freely and is so tidy that ground cover had to be provided for the ground coverer! The crimson Souvenir d'Alphonse Lavellée when pegged made a good contrast to Frau Karl Drushki, but as all crimson roses need good soil her personal preference was the 'rose of dreams' Roger de Lambelin, in dark crimson with a white edge. Baron Girod l'Ain, similarly coloured but coarser and easier, was planted with Souvenir du Docteur Jamain. She recognised the potential of the rugosa rose Frau Dagmar Hastrup in a wide border, but never planted it in her garden as a hedge, preferring it as an isolated plant. Several other rugosas, such as Max Graf, Paulii and Schneelicht, were good ground cover, but essentially for other people: Margery found their short flowering period unsuited to her concept of a flower for every day, and turned her mind to finding interesting ground cover for whatever roses she did plant – although, bearing Walter's early training in mind, she knew an exhibitor of roses, or enthusiasts for the formal rose garden, would not approve of her aims.

Her garden visiting gave her good ideas, as when she saw *Scilla sibirica*

on a cold morning, to be followed by grape hyacinths, chionodoxas and puschkinias. She knew that in William Robinson's garden at Gravetye low plants were allowed to soften the rose beds, and saw that Bodnant used the idea to great effect.

Her first choices were *Myosotis dissitiflora* with pink and white claytonia, or secondly the double-flowering chamomile, *Anthemis nobilis* (now *Chamaemelum nobile*) Flore Pleno, with pennyroyal. The planting was not as satisfactory as the idea, as they wandered too much. The rose bed became a home for seedlings of *Artemesia pedemontana*, *Chrysanthemum haradjanii* and once *Lychnis flos-jovis*. *Stachys lanata* kept down weeds and took little from the soil because of its shallow rooting; indeed *Ajuga reptans* and *reptans* Rubra would cover the soil more effectively than *Lamium maculatum*. In the longer term Margery felt that traditional cottage plants, such as periwinkle and violets, were a better background for roses than *Viola cornuta* and *cornuta* Alba, which are so much used.

In her lectures she often recommended the use of hostas with old roses, their large leaves suiting the situation better than geraniums and euphorbias; but when pressed on what her own preference would be, she returned to daisies and primroses – she could never have enough of these. She grew Dresden China and Rob Roy, she added pink Alice and The Pearl, but used the ground under her roses for the divisions of that favourite 'hen and chickens' daisy – which Parkinson called *Bellis minor hortensis prolifera*, the double fruitful daisy, or Jackanapes-on-horseback. Had the plants been available she would certainly have used the old double primroses: the demand for these in the nursery always outstripped the supply. Margery never created what she always hoped for, a tapestry of violets, primroses, daisies and pinks as a background for roses, but it remained an aim until her death.

IVY FOR GROUND COVER

She became extremely enthusiastic for ivies, and at one time grew over fifty different varieties. In the winter of 1954, a difficult one in Somerset gardens, when so much else was failing, the variegated ivies of Victorian breeding remained sleek and untouched by the frost. Her

favourite was *Hedera helix* Jubilee Gold Heart, with red stems and dark leaves with bright gold centres. She enjoyed the frilled parsley leaves of *Hedera helix* Cristata for winter picking for the house, but did not fare so well with the smaller silver-leaved ivies; *Hedera helix* Harold and an improved form of *Hedera helix* Chicago were the most satisfactory. Less distinct and with a broader leaf, *Hedera h.* Marmorata grew well enough, but the speckled leaves did not make the clear contrast and long trails of Silver Queen. *Hedera h.* Marginata Rubra has a beautiful mixture of grey-green, pale cream and pink, but it never made effective ground cover. It needed careful planting, like Heise with its congested leafy growth, and the variegated Sagittaefolia. Fascinated by these ivies, Margery created a mixed border in full sun of what to her was the perfect all-year ground cover. She grew *H.helix* Variegata Minor with Little Diamond, Iceberg, Fantasia and sub-Marginata.

She concluded Glacier was one of the best for silver and white ground cover, but found difficulty in deciding on the best gold ivy, principally because of nomenclature. Eventually she concluded that Buttercup was the same as *Hedera helix* Chicago Aurea and as Gold Cloud, which was also known as Russell's Gold.

For a medium-sized ivy she preferred *H.h.* Cristata, but for quick ground cover under trees Sagittaefolia, Feastii and the energetic Neilson were best. The five-lobed Welsh wood ivy *Hedera helix* Pedata is still found wild in Welsh woods and East Lambrook grew the variety Pedata Grey Arrow with a straight narrow version called Heron; these were blended with the strong-growing Irish ivy *H.h* Hibernica, though they proved better ground cover than the little congested ivies Congesta and Conglomerata. These looked better mixed with the large variegated *Hedera colchica* Dentata Variegata and *Hedera canariensis* Gloire de Marengo.

This interest in ivies was discovered at a fortunate time, as she was getting older; she often told her friends that if she could start again she might have designed a different garden for her old age. Informed use of ivy as ground cover reduced weeding, and also extended the winter colour in the garden, a theme pursued in her books *An All the Year Garden* and *A Flower for Every Day*. She wanted colour but not necessarily strong colour, allowing appreciation of the beauty of foliage in colours and texture.

GROUND COVER FOR ACID SOIL

It was probably this, and her view that English gardens were over-rosed and over-rhododendroned, which deterred her from growing azaleas and rhododendrons. She did grow *Rhododendron forrestii repens* in her first flush of enthusiasm for flowering ground cover, but never found the end result justified the effort of making special peat beds, top-dressing yearly with peat and keeping constantly moist. She continued to enquire from nurseries and friends if a good low-growing rhododendron could be found for ground cover; despite trials with several hybrids like *repens* Williamsianum and Blue Tit *(augustinii x impeditum)*, she eventually concluded that the best was *R.ferrugineum*, the alpenrose, which does not insist on lime-free soil. Its irregular growth was pleasant in the paved terrace, and offered what Margery liked in her favourite plants – not only a white form, but also a double-flowering crimson. She often conceded to questioners that there were many better growers of rhododendrons than she was; but she had achieved as much as any grower would given her alkaline soil.

Her interest in ground cover for acid soil, too, was constant, particularly in the gardens she visited in Devon and Cornwall. She once lectured in Cornwall on the most suitable plants for good ground cover she had seen on acid soils; a member of the audience later commented on the large variety she was able to include, keeping the interest of everyone present.

Cornus canadensis (creeping dogwood) was the most effective dogwood, with its flat rosettes of leaves about 6in from the ground. In June the slender stems hold out four large white petalloid bracts, and this is followed by a ruby-red berry in the centre, which enlivens the plant until the leaves turn gold. Needing light acid soil and moist shade, it grew with difficulty at East Lambrook. Her audience reaction when she suggested shortias and schizocodons as ground cover was not encouraging, but she had seen them in moist shade in Mr Hadden's garden at West Porlock – both *Schizocodon soldanelloides* Magnus and *Shortia uniflora* Grandiflora; she told the disbelievers to go and see for themselves. She agreed that *Epigaea repens* and *Linnaea borealis* were choosy plants that might not provide effective cover, but suggested

Dryas octopetala was the best linking plant for the two, growing in both sun and shade with its white golden-centred flowers.

Suitable woodland ground cover could be grown by using the dark shining leaves of *Galax aphylla* with the tiny *Iris lacustris*, but for sun *Lithospermum diffusum* Heavenly Blue was excellent, spreading quickly and flowering in May and June, its blue as vivid as any gentian's. Many of the best ground-cover plants are small and among these the whole family of gaultherias were excellent: she particularly recommended *procumbens* and *cuneata*, feeling that *nummularioides* did not show its dull pink flowers effectively; and she reminded her listeners that where well suited *Gaultheria shallon* could do for acid soil what *Hypericum calycinum* did for lime.

The damp-loving bog rosemary *Andromeda polifolia* never runs wild, but its 15in-square clumps do not give effective cover. *Ledum groenlandicum* ('Labrador tea') and *Leiophyllum buxifolium* were more reliable for ground cover, at 2 to 3ft high, the best carpeter being *Mitchella repens* ('Partridge berry'), with small pink flowers and dark green shiny leaves.

Margery concluded her ground cover on acid soil lecture with a warning: she would first make certain that the ground was free of all perennial weeds, and then take a long hard look at every available variety of heather. Those that make dense carpets, such as *Erica vagans* Mrs D.F. Maxwell and *Erica cinerea* C.D. Eason, could be combined not only to form a close-growing mat but also to provide what for her was essential, a pattern of flowers and leaf colour attractive every day of the year.

7

Use of Colour

Margery's attitude to colour in the garden had been influenced quite early in her gardening life by Mrs Clive Ponsonby Fane of Brympton d'Evercy and Phyllis Reiss at Tintinhull and she combined an artistic flair for all-year colour with an impeccable eye for a good plant. It was not until quite late in life that she started to consider separate gardens for specific colours and the challenge of mingling pure shades of blue or shades of white to flower throughout the year. Interest in green flowers probably began her work in creating single-colour flower gardens; she was intrigued by their use in Tudor and Stuart gardens.

Margery frequently lectured at length upon aspects of the use of colour in the garden, beginning by saying that everyone has a different taste for colour, and must create the blending that particularly pleased. She advocated avoiding bright colours because she felt most of her visitors wanted restful gardens; a problem she faced was that the lime in her soil made colours more intense. This led her always to want a background of green leaves and to rely on varying shades of foliage. In her early days a friend advised that if she did not know which colour to plant, she should choose a pastel shade, because that would always mix harmoniously. Margery found this advice infallible but used stronger colours with the pastels to add depth. For example, soft blue, lilac and pink needed stronger colour, and *Campanula glomerata* was added, with its deep blue heads; or the crimson rose Frensham could supply it, flowering above *Salvia sclarea* var. *turkestanica* near the hedge at the back of the border. A little shade deepened the colour of crimson flowers. A white dianthus, Thomas, grew against a mound of bronze-leaved fennel which was cut down to avoid flowering.

'There was a time when the criterion of a good garden was colour, and the vivid colour of massed flowers the main aim. We still want colour, but not necessarily strong colour. I am glad that we have come to appreciate the beauty of foliage in all its colours and textures,' she wrote in *An All the Year Garden*.

This view of the house, lawn and barton shows how coloured leaves were used to create an impression of flowers from a distance

The garden at East Lambrook had ample scope for colour experimentation. *Phlox decussata* grew better and flowered longer in shade or among shrubs, as did the dark red paeonies and the red oriental poppies. Beauty of Livermere was a form of *Papaver bracteatum* in pure blood-red without a hint of orange – orange being a colour generally excluded from the garden, although Margery had a weak spot for the double Welsh poppy, *Meconopsis cambrica* Flore Pleno. Lemony-orange flowers against a good green background created her pastel effect, and she did not allow house-room to the orange of *Hieracium aurantiacum*, 'Grim the Collier'. The orange red-hot pokers would be planted at the back of the border for autumn, to rise through a sea of green or be toned down by the purple leaves of *Acer platanoides*.

Yellow was used with care, the rich egg-yolk shades being subdued with white flowers or silver foliage. She liked Black-eyed Susan, *Rudbeckia fulgida*, and planted the rich gold variety Goldsturm between the Iceberg rose and *Helichrysum splendidum*: this blooms from July to September when the garden can be dull, and the yellow of the flowers is less strident because of the large black-coned centres. *Helenium autumnale*

Pumilum was a bright yellow dwarf which Margery used to like hidden in green, but she eventually decided the dark-centred Mme Canivet was a better mixer because the petals were paler and the dark centre added distinction. Greeny-yellow as a colour was welcomed almost anywhere. A pale yellow golden rod, *Solidago hybrida* Lemore, was grown with a tall lavender phlox, pale blue *Aster macrophyllus* and the off-white *Aster corymbosus (divaricatus)* with black whiplike stems.

Margery once grew a nearly-orange form of inula, and although she distributed it to acquaintances it has now apparently been lost. It grew more strongly than the type and one visitor remembered its large heart-shaped leaves in the green garden as a backdrop to eryngiums *agavifolium* and *pandanifolium (decaisneana)*.

Yellow and blue were not grown together; she would grow pink with deep blue and strong magenta with soft or pale shades of blue. This was surprising in someone who had read so carefully about Mrs Earle's and Gertrude Jekyll's plantings of colour before the First World War. One of the problems of planting at East Lambrook was to give depth to narrow borders, and blue which is essentially the artist's colour of distance could have been highlighted more dramatically to deepen the effect where large numbers of species of plants were grown.

Instead, this distance effect was achieved by using violet and purple with pale pink or acid and lime green, and purple foliage was a background for all the pastel colours Margery needed to accentuate a long-term planting. For much of her gardening life, under the influence of the silver and crimson planting at Brympton d'Evercy, silver carpets were planted under crimson, or a crimson underplanting made where silver foliage was massed. After her gardening became more acclaimed she changed to planting white and silver together, or glaucous leaves beneath crimson and purple. An example of this was *Phormium tenax* Purpureum surrounded by *Othonnopsis cheiriifolia*.

White Gardens

Margery had strong views about white gardens which became stronger as she grew older. She never planted them herself, feeling they would be too sophisticated for her garden, but as she travelled so widely she saw other people's mistakes and frequently lectured upon how she

would plant a white garden. There were three which she enjoyed: at Sissinghurst, Crathes Castle and Glyndebourne in that order. She frequently disagreed with Vita Sackville-West over her use of plants, particularly white roses, but agreed that the overall effect of the white garden at Sissinghurst was a great inspiration to many people, whereas she felt Crathes was a little too thin, and Glyndebourne's emphasis on evening light too stagey to be emulated in the gardens she was attempting to bring back to England. For white at East Lambrook she planted a group of Pacific delphiniums at the highest level of the terrace, with a big clump of the white long-flowering evergreen *Libertia grandiflora*, a white mallow to add another shape, and held the group together with the silver foliage of *Artemesia absinthium* Lambrook Silver. Another grouping was the rose Iceberg near a silver-variegated philadelphus and gladiolus, The Bride, using variegated bugle as ground cover to stop weeds. The variegated form of apple mint softened stiff and angular plants, while *Euonymus fortunei* Silver Queen was another plant commended to help a white scheme.

Anaphalis triplinervis is a neat little plant with its cushions of evergreen silver leaves. *Anaphalis margaritacea* was less silver but Margery liked its green leaves with darker foliage, and would let it smother the ground near *Campanula latifolia* Macrantha, philadelphus and eucryphia. *Anaphalis yedoensis (cinnamomea)* flowers later, at up to 3ft high. Great care was taken not to cut this plant before the spring because the willow-like leaves of grey, lined with silver, pleased her when rimed by frost. In her early gardening days she planted a great deal of perennial candytuft, *Iberis sempervirens*, and in one place where it still grows the *Anaphalis yedoensis* was backed by *Iris ochroleuca*, the whole kept tidy by cutting back the iris foliage as it yellowed in autumn.

Campanula persicifolia was planted in as many forms as possible, but because she was more interested in this as a cottage-type than a botanical flower, it was used in unexpected rather than planned planting. She frequently discussed the uses of roses which would romp away over trees, like *Rosa filipes* Kiftsgate, *Rosa longicuspis* or the Garland Rose, Sanders White. This last-named was planted to run over a small apple tree and it then used the purple-leaved sloe alongside. Margery was enthralled by the effect of a rectangular rose garden in Gloucestershire with Nevada flowering as a centrepiece in September, and also by a planting at one of the small gardens at Rowallane, the National Trust

garden in Northern Ireland, where *Viburnum plicatum tomentosum* was surrounded by stones to mark the centre of a small raised bed.

Margery became fascinated by this viburnum, placing several around the garden and recommending it widely. One planting which stayed within the garden and pleased her was the upright variety Rowallane placed by a hornbeam, with alpine strawberries, white *Cyclamen neapolitanum* and white colchicum. She found when lecturing a constant enquiry for white forms of familiar plants – white Judas trees (*Circis siliquastrum*), *Lychnis coronaria* Alba, nerines, schizostylis and *Iris unguicularis* Alba. This plant was always good for a five-minute digression at a heavy Women's Institute meeting when they would not listen to Margery's constant plea to treasure the plants in their own village gardens. Some white plants were what were termed stop-gaps: white *Thymus serpyllum*, the white *Liriope muscari*, *Santolina virens*, and for ground cover the white *Lamium maculatum* with *Prunella grandiflora* White Loveliness (self-heal); *Ajuga reptans*, white vincas and violets with *Bergenia Silberlicht*, and the primrose White Wanda, finishing with her favourite white flower the double white primrose.

GREEN GARDENS

Many green flowers did not fit into her usual seventeenth-century cottage gardens theme, some of the later introductions were far too sophisticated for that effect. But green flowers became more and more fashionable during Margery's gardening time and the original concept of a Stuart green garden had become almost an exotic green-flowered jungle by 1965. A wide range of unusual plants was added to the green garden so it became more generally interesting. Probably she was talking so often to Women's Institutes who had heard flower arrangers enthusing about green flowers that the green garden changed almost by accident. Its character was already changing when she first brought in the South American eryngiums with their spiky foliage and heads of soft green. She added kniphofia and the hardy palm *Trachycarpus fortunei*, with *Fatsia japonica* which flowerd in late autumn. The rather solid palm and fatsia combined well with eryngiums *pandanifolium, bromeliifolium, serra* and *agavifolium*.

She knew of few green-flowered shrubs to provide the bones for the

Cornus controversa variegata and *Prunus* Ukon use shape and leaves to soften the privy walls and roof

green garden, but used *Ribes laurifolium* with its greeny-white flowers in February, and *Bupleurum fruticosum*. The position was too exposed for *Garrya elliptica*, which was surprising, as it is now commonly grown much further north than Somerset.

The green rose remained, its flowers complementing the eryngium foliage, and the honeysuckle *Lonicera chaetocarpa* was trailed around the edge, its green and cream flowers opening in pairs up the stems. *Phlomis chrysophylla* was added to *Pittosporum tenuifolium*, while the Alexandrian laurel *Danae racemosa* with its glossy green arching stems looked well with the gold of *Philadelphus coronarius* Aureus and *Cassinia fulvida*, the 'golden heather'.

The herbaceous planting tended to be overshadowed by the alchemillas or lady's mantles, grown in various places in no less than five varieties – *mollis*, *vulgaris*, *alpina*, *conjuncta* and *erythrosora*. They were left behind from the early plantings, but their good-natured self-seeding saved the garden from its failures, of which *Bupleurum angulosum*, *Ixia viridifolia* and *Aquilegia viridiflora* were the principal losses. All had unusual green flowers and added an element of the exotic to the planting. Where failures

did occur the space was filled with astrantias.

To bring contrast, one or two other plants remaining from the original plantings survived. The greenish-yellow double buttercup *Ranunculus bulbosus* Pleniflorus and *Ornithogalum pyrenaicum*, with *Galtonia princeps*, were planted beneath the ivies Plume d'Or and Minima which acted as an effective foil and ground cover. In her enthusiasm for these green flowers, almost every corner was packed with an extra species: *Allium siculum* with green and maroon flowers, with hellebores *corsicus, sternii, foetidus* and *viridis;* *Tellima grandiflora* and *Heuchera viridis*, while *Mitella breweri* provided the ground cover.

The overall effect of the planting was almost plum-puddingy, heavily filling the ground, so some grasses were added – the tall *Miscanthus sinensis* Gracillimus, the grey-green *Miscanthus sacchariflorus*, with golden *Alopecurus pratensis* kept short and used as ground cover. Margery realised that this garden depended on many rather botanical species, some of which would flower and die. She kept a ready supply of seeds and plants of *Nicotiana* Lime Green, and *Zinnia* Envy to fill in where any disaster occurred.

Blue Flowers

The fact that no blue garden was made at East Lambrook was principally because of lack of a suitable site. The lime altered blue more markedly than any other colour, and Margery decided that she could not meet the colour pattern she wished to produce sufficiently well; the previously discussed complementary plantings of other shades were necessary.

The green garden, in particular, became part of the essence of surprise achieved at East Lambrook. 'The gardens that are remembered are those that lure you on. No one wants to linger in a garden that has no surprises, and if the whole garden can be seen at once there is a tendency to pay less attention to its treasures than if they were discovered in unexpected places', Margery wrote *(Gardening in the Shade)*. With her early potager design, visitors found themselves almost exclaiming aloud 'Whatever shall I find next?'

GOLD AND SILVER

Golden foliage was needed at East Lambrook, with so many areas of shade and the desire to make plants appear to be coming nearer or to be pushed further to the background by use of their contrasting heights. Golden marjoram, *Origanum vulgare* Aureum, proved the best close heavy mat of evergreen leaves, while the golden form of creeping Jenny, *Lysimachia nummularia* Aurea, lost its invasiveness if established on dry ground.

The golden mint, *Mentha gentilis* Aurea, is not evergreen but makes a thicket of foliage in the summer. Its roots run through a garden as strongly as those of the ordinary mint; so do the roots of the golden balm, *Melissa officinalis* Aurea, but this also seeded everywhere, defeating Margery's object of carefree gardening. Bowles' golden grass. *Milium effusum* Aureum, was grown for bright colour in shade in spring – but it seeded too widely and small pieces quickly became clumps. Foxtail, *Alopecurus pratensis* Foliis Variegata, made a good bronze show despite the untidy effect before the flower spikes came. The golden snowberry *Symphoricarpos orbiculatus* Variegatus, growing to about 3ft high as a specimen above lower ground plants, gave an attractive effect, with its small pointed leaves margined irregularly with gold. These golden shades contrasted well with glaucous plants, such as *Othonnopsis cheiriifolia*, with its flat paddle-shaped bluish leaves and yellow daisy flowers. It would fill its allotted place in the front of a border more quickly than the tidier-growing rue *(Ruta graveolens* Jackman's Blue). Her innumerable varieties of pinks covered the ground with glaucous-blue foliage. The Highland hybrids made excellent mats, as did Musgrave's Pink, and the Brympton Red pink, with single red, scented flowers, gave ground cover par excellence. For autumn colour, *Sedum spectabile*, its fleshy leaves making a compact rosette, provided one of the best-behaved plants in the garden. The palest colour comes from *Sedum spectabile* Rosea, taller than the type, but not comparable to the hybrids, such as Autumn Joy, Meteor, Carmen and Brilliant, which like *Sedum telephium* Munstead Red, made thick neat covers; *Sedum maximum atropurpureum* was looser in growth.

She liked the dwarf fescue *Festuca ovina glauca* grown with

Helictotrichon sempervirens, and a grass that grows taller, but is equally tidy if controlled, *Elymus arenarius*; it increased so fast on poor soil it became a most efficient ground cover, with its 4ft stems and stiff flower-spikes. Having seen *Acaena adscendens* planted in contrast with *Sedum maximum atropurpureum* on a broad terrace, she used acaena with scarlet *Lobelia fulgens*.

THE SILVER GARDEN

She felt that greeny-blues were complementary with gold or crimson, but that with silver leaves or variegation these colours had a deadening effect; although silver-leaved plants were useful, they were better left to themselves. After several visits to Hidcote, she decided that a small garden of silver-leaved plants on a dry south bank of the garden would make a perfect foil to the green-flowered garden she had planted on the high ground above the barton entrance.

The planting of the silver garden was planned with care. It was not an original idea – before planting she looked at the crimson and silver plantings at Brympton d'Evercy, and more particularly the white and silver garden at Tintinhull. Margery used *Stachys lanata* (lamb's lugs) as her staple plant here for its reliable silver-leaved effect, and in full sun the creeping *Artemisia lanata (pedemontana)*, whose thick silver carpet she had admired at Knightshayes, Tiverton.

The gaps left between evergreen rosettes of silver plants needed careful filling. One plant used was *Anaphalis triplinervis* for its neat silver foliage and also its small ivory daisies in late summer. *Lychnis coronaria* has flannelly leaves some 5 to 6in long, and as a good cottage plant was in keeping with the effect she wanted in the silver garden. She grew the magenta-flowered one and the crimson Abbotswood Rose, as a contrast to the white flowers, and the very rare form of white with a pink centre. The other lychnis used was *L.flos-jovis* Cottage Maid, but this had not the long-flowering habit of *L.coronaria*, and it needed a sure touch in its placing.

For height, *Verbascum bombyciferum* was used as a dot plant, and an arresting group of the cotton thistle *Onoporadon acanthium* made a brilliant winter centrepiece: with 12ft stems and a 6ft span, these thistles needed careful placing.

VARIEGATED AND TRICOLOUR FORMS

For leaf colour and form, it is surprising that she did not use the variegated and tricoloured pelargoniums. Variegation or tricolour form is however difficult to place in a garden, and many of the plants are neither as hardy nor as reliable as the type of the species. *Hypericum x moserianum* was one such plant Margery enjoyed but never found quite successful. Its leaves of cream, emerald and crimson betray the reason: any red in a variegated leaf is almost a warning of impending doom and the plant must be kept in perfect health to achieve the type of growth Walter had trained her to expect from her plants. A tricolour that performed better was *Salvia officinalis* Tricolor, in purple, cream and magenta pink, making spreading mounds which yielded plenty of cuttings for the nursery, as would the tricolor *Ajuga reptans* Rainbow.

Using variegated plants for ground cover is not the easiest way of gardening: it is almost a contradiction in terms. In a variegated leaf only about 50 per cent of the photosynthesis likely in a green leaf can take place, so the plant will be less vigorous and suffer intrusion from its next-door neighbour. She did find, though, that several variegated-leaved plants, such as *Euonymus radicans* Silver Queen, are evergreen and tough and make reasonably spreading ground cover, even though they do not grow as quickly as the type. *Lamium maculatum* Variegatum she found too exuberant and needed controlling.

Two plants with interesting leaves that made effective variegat-ed ground cover were *Arum italicum* Pictum and *Arum italicum* Marmoratum. The berries of these 'lords-and-ladies' are not for a garden where children play, but the leaves are attractive over dry shade in spring. *Cardamine aurea* was originally an annual proposition, but mildly seeded through the garden making an effective cover of gold-splashed leaves in rounded hummocks.

A good plant used for special effect in winter was the variegated figwort *Scrophularia aquatica* Variegata; at that time of year it makes large handsome rosettes, of sparkling cream on green. Later in the year

Clematis were used in situations where many gardeners would grow roses. Here
Clematis The President entwines the front door lamp

the flower-spike covers the leaves but by that time the garden was full of flowers and the rosette was not missed. The variegated blackberry was growing as ground cover at the top of the ditch, with pink pampas-grass behind, and a Ballawley Hybrid bergenia on the other side. When the blackberries were scarlet the planting looked its best, but the bergenia's crimson leaves made a magnificent contrast when the blackberries were over.

CONIFERS FOR STRONG EFFECT

Many gardeners at this time started to form collections of variegated plants. Margery, with her eye for colour and form, rejected the thought of variegation for its own sake; she used these plants for general effect in the foreground, with dark conifers as ground cover behind. She liked hard-wearing, colourful conifers: a good prostrate conifer covering the soil at corners of borders, where the paving ran beside the bed, gave a feeling of spaciousness and stability and created the correct ambience of permanence.

An example of her choice is *Juniperus chinensis (J.x davurica)* Expansa Variegata, horizontal in growth and bright green with white tips to the branches. It started as a 6in plant at the bottom of the sundial, eventually covering a wide space and working its way up the column. There is nothing flimsy about conifers, and their effect is pleasing throughout the year. Her insistence on the permanency needed in good plantings contributed substantially to the widespread planting of conifers today. She was sufficiently foresighted to realise that with the countryside becoming alien territory for birds, their chance of survival would improve if every garden planted at least one conifer.

She did not advise the mat-forming *Juniperus conferta (litoralis)* in a small neatly planted garden, preferring it in a woodland setting. For more important spaces *Juniperus communis saxatilis (nana)*, with its flat grey-green branches was planted. In gardens where something larger and higher was required she advised *Juniper chinensis (J. x media)* Pfitzerana, contrasting it with its varieties of Aurea and Glauca. The dwarf ground-covering conifers were not planted to excess in her own garden, where she preferred the stronger cones of her 'pudding trees' (*Chamaecyparis lawsoniana* Fletcheri).

8

Gardening on Clay and Lime

Of the strands woven to create the garden at East Lambrook Manor, gardening on clay and lime was probably the most unusual. Ground cover was used in many gardens, and though her use of cottage-garden plants and 'florist' flowers could be considered unusual, many people had grown winter flowers before. Gardening seriously on clay and lime, and in the shade, at a time when acid-loving rhododendrons, azaleas and rock plants, under the influence of Farrer, were fashionable, was adventurous.

Margery and Walter had bought East Lambrook Manor and then found that the soil was not suitable to create what at that time was considered an attractive fashionable garden. The way that she used her years of experience was original and in recording her successes, she was equally truthful about her failures: more of those resulted from growing plants on clay than from growing them in shade.

Good clay is a sound basis for herbaceous paeonies and delphiniums, but poor for most bulbs because of the lack of drainage. The two acres of East Lambrook offered a wide variety of terrain, but bulbs – and lilies in particular – were not generally successful.

The first rule she adopted was always to work to improve the texture of the soil. Her good neighbourliness was of immense importance; by talking to local people she learned the age-old rule to work with the soil, not against it. An additional reason to break parts of the garden into smaller compartments of individual flowers was that the heavy clay could then be worked from a path. 'One of the first things I learnt when I started gardening on heavy clay soil was never to walk on it when it was wet', she wrote *(Gardening on Clay and Lime)*. Any odd-shaped broken tiles and irregular stones were laid down to achieve informality throughout the whole garden and take the weight of the every-increasing numbers of visitors. Experience proved clay was better cultivated for the top 10in and made very fertile, leaving the larger plants a firm foothold.

Early in gardening at East Lambrook she adopted the technique of

planting shrubs and trees which never varied thereafter. The hole for any permanent plant was filled with sand, peat and compost, and watered in afterwards to get it round the roots. The base was filled with upside-down turves. For plants with big roots, the whole would be 2ft square. The flower beds were never dug: firstly there was not room, secondly it disturbed the crops of self-sown seedlings, important for the nursery and thirdly by mulching with compost, peat or even lawn cuttings the worms were encouraged to keep the top soil open and help it create its own fertility. 'A garden on clay can be good if the clay is made workable; a garden on lime can be as good as any garden in the land if the garden sticks to the plants that like lime.'

THE COMPOST MULCH

One good way of keeping heavy clay moist, even in the driest weather, was to have a good cover of growing plants. This led her into the type of gardening she described in *Ground Cover Plants* and *Carefree Gardening*. Where she was unable to plant very closely, she considered a mulch was as good as a can of water every day – particularly for primroses and cyclamen, two plants which gained much of their moisture from heavy dews. The mulch presented the flowers more attractively to the visitor, and also there were fewer annual weeds.

This routine steadily improved the quality of the soil at East Lambrook over the thirty years in which Margery gardened there, and she became an addict to the compost heap. Everything suitable, from newspapers to straw bales to egg shells and tea leaves, went onto it. She was lucky in having loyal help from Jean Gascombe and Maureen Whitty in the garden, but she even tried their patience on one occasion. She had been out lecturing and on her return was told that Jean's nose had been profusely bleeding. 'But what did you do with the blood?' asked Margery. 'Put it on the compost heap I hope.' Margery was fortunate that these two ladies and Jean Burgess were available to help her at times throughout her gardening years. After 1960 as she became more and more involved with her writing and lecturing, they undertook the donkey-work of maintaining the garden, receiving its guests, and the increasing correspondence entailed in lecturing and plant identifications.

A two-year programme was eventually settled on for the composting,

on the principle that the bigger the heap, the better the compost. Margery maintained that no part of the garden should be untidy, and after experimenting with a concrete base, rejected it because it discouraged worms. A walled enclosure of double trimmed turves was rejected for having too many untidy grass whiskers. Eventually, her compost heaps were enclosed by bales of straw, two bales high enclosed by posts and wire. The straw could be used to start the base of the second heap, to be followed by a good 6in of garden waste. A layer of about half the quantity of farmyard manure was then covered with wood ash, lime and burnt soil. These layers were repeated, with a generous layer of farmyard manure before the last layer of wood ash and earth. The top was then covered with hay, strewn loosely to keep in the moisture and heat; pieces of pipe were thrust into the heap to allow the air to penetrate and facilitate rapid rotting by bacteria.

As the general level of soil fertility improved, so the weeds in the garden increased. She never attributed this to the use of green annual weeds in the compost, but felt that she was creating better conditions for the survival of weed seedlings. She looked forward to the season when the herbaceous plants could be cut down, and there were spaces between the shrubs and evergreens: she could then start spreading the previous year's compost, making sure every plant received its share, keeping it well away from plants that do best in poor soil. The compost was full of worms, which rapidly pulled it into the soil, so by the spring it was fully incorporated. She always used a board or kneeler when planting, so the ground was not compacted by trampling.

Margery's string of golden rules for planting would, if observed, have made planting possible on only one day of the year. She even went to the trouble of buying plants from a nursery with soil similar to her own; she felt that otherwise the shock of the change was too much to allow some plants to settle down with her. A less dedicated gardener could consider her over-fastidious, but few gardeners have had so many plants chosen for photographs as well-grown examples of their species – even now, thirty years since she was gardening at East Lambrook.

Part of her success was that she dropped plants that did not like her garden. Among these were *Scabiosa caucasica*, pyrethrums, platycodon, pulsatillas, eryngiums, *Arnebia echioides* and *Tropaeolum speciosum*.

LILIES AND ROSES ON CLAY

Lilies were one of the bulbs which usually did not like East Lambrook. In Margery's time the new American hybrids with their stronger constitution were not widely available. The Bellingham hybrids, the most recent then introduced, succeeded in raised beds, as did *Lilium regale* and *L.szovitzianum*. Asiatic species still commanded respect, but *martagon*, *candidum* and *pyrenaicum*, the standby lilies of English gardens for 400 years, were not considered the best choices. The emphasis was still on *Lilium auratum*, rhododendrons and azaleas. When Margery first went to East Lambrook a few *Lilium candidum* were growing; she moved them to better drainage, did not disturb them again and they grew more strongly. It was a great pity she did not pursue her interest in lilies further, and save the unfashionable double-flowered forms of *candidum* and *martagon*, or grow the variegated-leaved *candidum*. These flowers survive, but only just; George Morrison Taylor knew of them in larger numbers than we can conceive today.

There was a similar hesitance in her treatment of roses, as already seen. Her views on roses are central to her whole theme of planting at East Lambrook. Clay soil is reputed to grow good roses because of the water retention, but Margery did not enjoy hybrid tea roses grown in beds with no underplanting: she thought there was no flower more beautiful and satisfying than a rose, but that the bushes themselves were only bearable in full leaf and covered with flowers. Therefore she used roses as any other plant, to decorate the garden. For example the velvet crimson Frensham was set against the soft blue of a Michaelmas daisy, or the elegant mauve of Sterling Silver against achillea Cerise Queen, *Salvia officinalis* Purpurascens (purple sage) against Magenta, or the flat Bourbon flowers of Rosemary rose against *Euphorbia pilosa* Major with its flat green heads of flowers. Pink floribundas with strong colour would be surrounded by flowers of dull slate-blue like *Malva sylvestris* Primley Blue and *Catananche caerulea* Major.

One of her personal dislikes was the use of a white floribunda such as Iceberg, massed in a large bed, but she used this rose frequently in a different way, planting it with *Artemesia* Lambrook Silver and *Iris* Paper Moon, or with *Centaurea gymnocarpa*; the yellow flowering

season would be extended with *Aconitum lycoctonum (A.vulparia)* and black-eyed Susan (rudbeckia).

Climbing roses were very successful. Those chosen by Margery and Walter when they first went to East Lambrook grew well and added an unfashionable charm to the walls. Autumn-flowering Lady Hillingdon, Mme Abel Chatenay and Gloire de Dijon were the standbys, but even the single pink Complicata was admired for its healthy growth over the old roof of the adjoining cottage. None was more loved than *Rosa longicuspis*: when Vita Sackville-West visited one September, looking for ideas to extend the autumn flowering range of her own garden, Margery told her that she wished to cover an old pear tree and two apple trees with flowers. Vita persuaded Margery, rather against her will, to use this rose – Vita was then at the height of her species-rose enthusiasm. Three cuttings of *longicuspis* arrived in a packet the following January, and Margery literally pushed them in the ground as Vita suggested. Their subsequent growth was a source of great joy, one of her most successful extensions of the flowering season.

'CLEMATIS ARE PLANTED NORTH AND GROW SOUTH'

Clematis were used in situations where most people would use roses, and on East Lambrook's heavy clay the same rules of planting applied. Broken brick, old manure, and a mixture of soil, sand and peat ensured success, provided the plants were tapped out of the pot and the roots fully extended. By following Walter's advice – planting deeply, mulching with manure and watering in drought – she succeeded with a whole range of cultivars which in his lifetime he would not let her grow. She always planted clematis on the north side of a tree or wall, to protect the stem from hot sun. Walter, it may be remembered, insisted on training his *Clematis jackmanii* with military precision; Margery preferred to pinch out the growing points in early spring and let the plants find their own support in the company of the plants they chose.

She trained *Clematis jackmanii* Superba over the wall near the garden gate, and it then made its way to the top of the wall, clothed the other side with blossoms, and scrambled into a bird cherry growing alongside. Obviously the blue and white *Clematis florida bicolor* (Sieboldii), beautiful

but difficult, would not put up with this treatment, but many of the small-flowered species showed up well on shrubs which flowered at a different time of year. The various hybrids of *C.texensis* were particularly good for this: the urn-shaped flowers of pink Duchess of Albany looked well woven through *Osmanthus delavayi*, and into some of the clumps of purple sage. Gravetye Beauty was given *Cornus controversa* Variegata, the dogwood with horizontal branches. Etoile Rose did not suit hebe, and Margery decided its habit and colour would be better in a Judas tree. *Clematis flammula* seeded itself effectively into an alder tree, while *viticella* was planted into another large bush of variegated cornus. The seeding habit of *C.flammula* made it a dangerous plant, but a seedling growing into the single pink rose Cupid on a pillar made a cloud of cream around it with the added advantage of the rose's strong perfume.

HERBACEOUS PLANTS FOR CLAY

As an inexperienced gardener, and before she began to plant borders and develop her themes of colour and duration of flowering, Margery had noticed the species which grew well on neighbours' heavy clay. First in this category were the campanulas, and of these *Campanula latiloba* with its 3 to 4ft spikes of open bells in blue or white, was able to grow anywhere strongly, and became recommended in her lectures; she grew the species and two improved forms in darker blue, Highcliffe and Percy Piper. She would frequently develop the theme of campanulas, because they fitted her concept of old cottage flowers. Also good for clay was *Campanula lactiflora*, with its soft milky-blue flowers and pleasant habit of self-seeding. The large heads of small flowers mixed well in the summer garden and were not too sophisticated for the wild garden. She preferred the pale pink Loddon Anna to the dark blue of Superba or Prichard's Variety, and used the dwarf Pouffe as an edging or in front of smaller plants. For hanging bells she liked the larger and more unusual Burghaltii, which flowers through summer and into autumn with flowers of dull slaty-blue.

Campanula glomerata or Jerusalem violet was again an old English type of plant, needed in the garden. Purple Pixie, a deep violet colour, was planted in arresting clumps in the middle of the border; the

Lysichitum americanum enjoyed the clay and lime in the ditch. Looking towards the malthouse in spring

white form was insufficiently strong growing. In 1960 Margery and I corresponded over the relative difficulty of growing the double white *Campanula persicifolia* Fleur de Neige on her soil and how she usually managed the smaller flowered Moerheimii; I supplied her with several cuttings. The weaker forms of *Campanula persicifolia* seem to need good drainage, very fertile soil and winter shelter to acquit themselves well. Drainage in the winter was a frequent problem at East Lambrook. The ordinary single blue and white forms of *Campanula persicifolia* would self-seed there, and were preferred to Telham Beauty and Snowdrift, the commercial varieties of the time. Beauty of Exmouth was grown for its soft double blue flowers, but Margery preferred the white in the cup-and-saucer form; she wrote dozens of letters in search of the blue cup-and-saucer form, however, and it became a precious plant for her, even though its flowers lacked the grace of the white and were difficult to place in the border.

Campanula poscharskyana was rampant enough to verge on becoming a weed. Planted on a wall where its long trail of light blue flowers

could hang down, it became less invasive. Again Margery preferred the white-flowered form for its less invasive properties, although it did not flower quite as long as the blue.

Anemones did well, in particular the Japanese, like the white Louise Uhink planted against a dark background; one group at East Lambrook had the yellow *Clematis rehderiana* as its backdrop. The pink and rose anemones grown gave more pleasure to visitors than to Margery. *Anemone japonica* was never as invasive as *hupehensis* which she always feared would colonise her borders. *Anemone nemorosa* (wood anemone) was a complete success, growing very strongly on the clay in several cultivars – the single white and the blue Robinsoniana, the double Alba Plena and one with coloured bracts. Striking success was achieved by preparing a special deep bed for the thong-like roots of *Anemone sulphurea (Pulsatilla alpina* var. *sulphurea)*, with its pasque-like flowers of pale yellow.

These and similar anemones were combined with primroses. She last flowered the double crimson Madame de Pompadour in 1960, when Mrs Emerson of The Leeke, Limavady, Ireland, had sent a particularly fine stock to England, but no primroses are truly perennial. Sometimes the hose-in-hose, sometimes the jack-in-the-green did better, and they needed care. Margery never tired of finding different ways to try to please them. She was the first to realise that modern breeders were making primroses and polyanthus too big and she clung to the older varieties she considered worth distribution.

Hellebores were a success on the clay. In the wild they grow in positions where a primrose would grow, but their habit is truly perennial. Most of the species, which were becoming popular for flower arranging, as well as a whole range of hybrids of *orientalis*, the Lenten rose, were grown. She had at one time no less than sixty named varieties of this plant and was a great populariser of its virtues in early spring.

Some of the gentians grew well, too. *Gentiana acaulis* in particular would grow, but not flower, in profusion; the August-flowering *Gentiana septemfida* in darker blue was reliable, but the growth of the willow gentian *Gentiana asclepiadea* in pure clay in the ditch garden was a source of great joy. The blue and white forms grew under the willow trees, but the blue and white striped form – which she called 'bicolour' – was a particular success. They were grown with carefully placed epimediums, whose dainty flowers in the spring, and colourful foliage through the

9

Gardening in the Shade

At the latitude of East Lambrook, by making maximum use of the available sunlight it is possible to obtain 5 tonnes per acre of vegetable dry matter each year: if anyone had attempted to describe gardening in these terms, Margery would have called it nonsense. She loved her plants, and packed them in; and as she wished to grow shrubs, and have the walls covered with creepers, this entailed finding some which would grow in the shade. When faced with a gardening problem, she would experiment to the point of trying five different plants to find just one for the position required. She rapidly acquired a wide knowledge of plants that would grow in the shade cast by other plants or created by the terrain of the garden. This knowledge was used to great effect with ground-cover plants, and she soon found that gardening in the shade was one of her most popular lecture subjects.

It is a measure of her pioneering spirit that her book *Gardening in the Shade* was among the first written specifically on the subject, and it was with plants for shade that she was most successful as a plantswoman. Once she began to garden with shade in mind, she realised many plants she had used for ground cover or out of season could equally be used for a shady situation; the soil could be adapted and improved to suit the plants required – her children must be correctly put to bed! Most plants in shade need soil with a high humus content, and hers were grown in soil of better than average fertility. Even so, there were of course some failures – a group that did not grow satisfactorily were the deep-rooted *Adonis amurensis*, *volgensis* and *vernalis*, with the allied *Hepatica triloba* and *acutiloba*. The clay at East Lambrook did not allow the roots to penetrate the second and third spits of soil, as they must for free flowering.

A SHADY BORDER

It is, of course, easier for a shady border to be full of flower in spring than in autumn, particularly if there is plenty of moisture. Flowering can start in January and continue full of interest, if carefully planted, until midsummer. The first flowers of the year are usually hellebores, and Margery planted the early-flowering *atrorubens* and *olympicus* with the flat greenish-white flowers of *orientalis*. No one has found a satisfactory way of moving *Helleborus niger*, but by growing her plants rapidly she was able to propagate the large early-flowering Potter's Wheel, with St Brigid and Ladham's Variety. She never managed to find the double-flowering variety of Christmas rose. Hellebores should be grown as separate clumps, so each plant makes a separate picture of flowers and leaves; these can be dotted about in odd places rather than set in a shady border. She preferred to place them so that they could be looked up to when in flower – particularly the *guttatus* hybrids.

The collection of hellebores at one time numbered over 200 varieties and species. *Helleborus foetidus* in the upright Italian form was planted as light shade for double primroses. In addition to the more sprawling native form, she also grew a dark-flowered one collected by E.A. Bowles in the Roja valley, with one from Mount Olympus and a further variety which came from a Shropshire garden.

Helleborus corsicus was a particular favourite, with its trusses of apple-green flowers, although it flopped around: when Phyllis Reiss at Tintinhull used it as a feature of a shady border, she staked the plants. Margery found a little staking at flowering time was satisfactory under a shady wall. Its light grey-green leaves made it as satisfying as the dark green *foetidus*. A clump of *lividus* would then be planted as a contrast; the first two would shelter the *lividus*, so that in passing on a fine day in early spring the scent could be enjoyed.

The small green-flowered *viridis* with its anemone-sized flowers was not evergreen. Like *torquatus* in dull grey-green, it lost its leaves for the two winter months when Margery felt the shady garden needed green

Shade from the hedge of *Lonicera nitida* sheltered the corms of *Cyclamen neapolitanum album*. *Angelica archangelica* is behind

leaves most. *Olympicus* was the first to flower, in October; followed by *atrorubens*, the red Christmas rose, in November, and then *kochii* and *odorus* by Christmas. Then came *H.niger* and *colchicus*, followed by *antiquorum* and *orientalis*, with the numerous named *orientalis x guttatus* hybrids. These crosses came in a wide colour range, through greeny-yellow to white, pink, crimson and black; at one time there were over 60 named varieties. With their respective colourings it would have been impossible to select their parentage. Nowadays we expect to see sophisticated *orientalis* seedlings, but at this time Margery's use of hellebores was unequalled since the 1880s. Various growers had produced individual named hybrids, such as Prince Rupert, Ballard's Black and Coombe Fishacre Purple, but to grow a wide-ranging long-season collection during the winter was new.

From this point in the year gardening in dull shade becomes increasingly easy. Pulmonarias, in blue, white, pink and red, were essentially forms of *Pulmonaria officinalis* and the gentian-blue *angustifolia*. Yellow could be added by *Doronicum austriacum*, and the dwarf *Hacquetia epipactis*. Spring bulbs and primroses were grown among the taller perennials, which gave them shade later in the year. By April, *Dicentra spectabilis* in pink and white took over, mixed in with aquilegias such as *alpina*, Hensol Harebell and many of the species used to create the then very fashionable long-spurred Mrs Scott Elliott strain. Margery felt that although these were more decorative, the older granny's bonnets suited her garden better.

They mixed well with the wall linaria, particularly the soft pink form Canon Went, and the heucherellas with their shell-pink flowers and light green leaves. Margery had a great fondness for the variety Bridget Bloom, because of her friendship with its progenitor, Alan Bloom of Bressingham; he frequently stayed at East Lambrook and was amazed at the way Margery would give him a fork before he left and say 'Go out and help yourself to any plant you care for'. *Heuchera rubescens* and *viridis* would be mixed with *Tellima grandiflora* and the large salmony-orange *Geum rivale* Leonard's Variety.

At one time she considered making a shade border of campanulas only, but felt the colour range of blue and white too limiting. Probably her favourite was the bright purple Jerusalem violet, *Campanula glomerata* but *persicifolia* with its numerous single and double garden forms ran it a close second.

Campanulas *lactiflora*, *latifolia*, *Burghaltii*, *van houttei* and *punctata* were added; and she enjoyed the small heart-shaped leaves of *alliariifolia*, and its creamy bells which would occasionally flower until December. *C.pyramidalis* is of course better used as a biennial, but she grew it perennially as a wall plant. Its hybrid with *C.versicolor*, known as x *pyraversii*, only 2ft high, was more reliably perennial. *Campanula trachelium* was grown in its single and double, blue and white, forms but without enthusiasm. With its neat nettle-like leaves and uninvasive habit this plant ought to have been one of her treasures. It is after all probably the old Canterbury Bell of Chaucer, doubtfully native; Gerard knew of it growing near Coventry, where it was called Coventry Bell. *Campanula medium* usurped its place in history. She allowed the invasive *Campanula rapunculoides* to grow almost wild throughout the garden, and once served the roots sliced with meat at a dinner-party, as the Elizabethans did.

Platycodons were added to the campanula corner in blue, white and pink, single and double flowers, but her real treasure was a hose-in-hose pink form of a cross between *Platycodon grandiflorus* and *apoyama*, which rarely increased but extended colour in this corner until late September. Towards the end of spring, she used the soft lavender and cream of *Thalictrum aquilegiifolium* with its soft grey-green leaves, because it filled an awkward flowering period, carrying the shady border into summer. *Adiantifolium* with its green flowers was carefully controlled, but the taller, later-flowering yellow of *speciosissimum* in its varieties of *sphacrocephalum* and Illuminator were always welcome. The lavender and white forms of *dipterocarpum* grow well in light shade and deep rich soil. The deep purple of the 5ft Hewitt's Double was a great joy in August, leading with the hardy geraniums to the later summer and autumn flowers for shade.

She tended to be swept along by her friends in her use of hardy geraniums; gardeners like A.T. Johnson and Vita Sackville-West grew them as ground cover. With their wide colour range she could not resist growing them in situations where other plants would be better.

Obviously *Geranium pratense* was happiest in the ditch garden, but after visiting Sissinghurst and seeing the double purple geranium in the violet garden, the double white, double blue and double purple were added to the shadier parts of the terrace garden, with *Geranium endressii*, both Wargrave Pink and Rose Clair varieties.

Geranium renardii with its dull grey-green leaves was usually planted against red or dark leaves, and *traversii* Russell Prichard planted where it could hang down and carry on flowering through into the autumn. *Ibericum* and *alpinum* were essentially plants for the wilderness. Two which Margery saw growing in the Savill Gardens, Windsor, and brought in out of the wild were *delavayi* and *wallichianum* Buxton's Blue, planted for contrast with *grevilleanum*.

Geranium sanguineum in pink and white gave its icing-sugar effect to an edging, and a long flowering period. Margery preferred the deep rose which Phyllis Reiss grew at Tintinhull beneath the ilex, providing colour in the shade as high summer turned to autumn. Not many plants could help in shady sites through this period, but *Cephalaria tatarica (gigantea)* in yellow, *Chelone barbata* in red, and *Cynoglossum nervosum* in blue were three plants normally grown in the sun which provided colour. *Dracocephalum pratii*, *Nepeta* Souvenir d'André Chaudron, *Lindelofia longiflora* and *Echinacea purpurea*. The King provided more blue. September brought the first *Anemone japonica* flowers.

UNCOMMON PLANTS WITH GARDEN PERSONALITY

Never satisfied with growing easy popular plants, and believing her public wanted to see less well-known cultivars and species, she experimented widely. Her clay soil allowed her several successes among plants expected to be difficult. *Saxifraga fortunei* is a woodland plant with a bad reputation, but she grew it in moist heavy soil and shade, and its late autumn flowering was a great success. *Iris innominata* grew well in moderate shade, its tangerine-yellow flowers netted with chocolate lines.

The eucomis family were widely considered half-hardy during the 1950s, with their South African origin and exotic appearance like pineapples. The green and purple flowers of *Eucomis bicolor* were successful in the green-flowered garden, however, and Margery then grew both *punctata* and *regia*, so well that their flowering stems would snap in strong wind.

Looking to the terraces past the malthouse and the ditch
The changing textures of the foliage softened the line of the path

A green flower with which she experimented was *Alstroemeria psittacina*. This beautiful flower in green and crimson originating from Brazil has always been considered marginally hardy, but for thirty years it grew on the same ledge in the rock garden. The Ligtu hybrids in shades of pink, buff, champagne and flame were grown in south-facing beds. *Aurantiaca*, with its reputation of being positively ineradicable, was never planted.

Fascicularia (Rhodostachys) bicolor with its bright blue October pincushion flowers and reputation of being fertilised by humming birds was an exotic from the Andes that settled happily at East Lambrook, providing interest (and blue colour) for visitors at a difficult time of year. Not so tropical in appearance and less free-flowering were *Hedychium densiflorum* (a 'ginger lily') and *Cautleya spicata* Robusta, but their leaves were sufficiently different to consider the space well used.

Eremurus was not grown at East Lambrook – after the one plant there was devoured by slugs. Margery enjoyed eremurus in the right setting, and perhaps she did not persevere sufficiently. As a source of surprise, some of the Highdown Hybrids, with their pastel colours of yellow, orange, pink and white, provide a haze of colour in early summer; an alternative but slightly more difficult planting would be the Japanese toad lilies, tricyrtis. Margery started a fashion for these woodland plants, which flower in late September; they needed time to establish but accepted more shade than *Salvia patens*. She preferred *Tricyrtis macropoda* in deep lilac with black blotches, and also grew *latifolia* and *stolonifera* in purple and mauve. *Hirta* in pale green, and *hirta* Alba in white, although smaller and less strong-growing it gave a good colour range for an unusual woodland species.

Two other plants included for entertaining visitors were *Hacquetia epipactis* and *Liriope muscari*. Hacquetia, also known as dondia, was the flower of Eleanour Sinclair Rohde's spring where green turned into gold, with its small gold flowers surrounded by a Elizabethan ruff of green shamrock leaves. *Liriope muscari* was another plant used to fill the awkward September to November gap. With its grassy ever-green leaves and bright lilac bells of muscari form, it never failed to please in a narrow bed facing north, under a hedge.

Looking towards the Malthouse, with verbascum, roses and alchemilla

AUTUMN IN THE SHADE

To Margery, autumn began in the shade with the flowering of the japonica anemones. Her particular favourite was the pure white Honorine Joubert – which here eclipsed the semi-double Louise Uhink. The pink ones offered a wider selection, from *Anemone hupehensis* to deep pink Prince Henry and Bressingham Glow. In silver-pink, which she liked to mix with the white *vitifolia robustissima*, Queen Charlotte was probably the best variety; while the narrow petals of the double pink Margarete were an especial joy. These tall anemones needed good dwarf plants for association. *Viola cornuta* in white, purple and mauve was used, while *gracilis*, shorter and neater, came to the front, in several named varieties such as Black Knight, Martin in bright purple, Nora Leigh in lavender-mauve and Haslemere in pinky-mauve. The yellow Moonlight and orange-green Irish Molly were not sufficiently strong-growing for these conditions; these and the fancy show violas were given a special situation in light shade in a moister part of the garden.

In the difficult August-September period in the shady border, sidalceas and hemerocallis also brought flower colour. The silver-pink of *Sidalcea malviflora* Rev Page Roberts was welcome in any of her colour schemes: it had the added bonus that its seedlings came true. Crimson Beauty and the medium-pink Sussex Beauty were added to an unusual hose-in-hose form. Their light foliage contrasted well with the day lilies (hemerocallis) which were becoming popular in America at this time. Margery grew orange *fulva*, and a favourite with double flowers and variegated foliage which she was given by E.A. Bowles; also pale lemon *citrina*, Hyperion in the same colour for its scent, Greengold and some of the early pinks like Pink Charm and Pink Lady. Nowadays, her collection of these early hybrids could be considered eccentric, but when grown in the shady borders, they were very progressive gardening.

As the season passed, *Monarda didyma* (bergamot) came into its own in moist shade – the species as well as Cambridge Scarlet. Few of the named varieties remain available for long: Croftway Pink and Mauve Queen are still just in commerce, but most of the other varieties have

Senecios, euphorbias, bergenia and *chrysanthemum parthenium aureum*

apparently disappeared. Snow Maiden and Mrs Perry in deep pink widen the colour range, with Mahogany and Blue Stocking enabling a successful border to keep alive. All bergamots need moisture and a good top dressing of peat or sawdust to help them through the winter.

Similar conditions suit herbaceous lobelias. *Lobelia fulgens* in full sun was too showy for East Lambrook, but in shade the crimson became almost sumptuous. Margery preferred green-leaved *Lobelia cardinalis*, but it never grew as well as the crimson-leaved varieties. The blue *syphilitica* was as reliable as its white form; *Lobelia x vedrariensis* was planted as much for its easy growth and resistance to frost as its violet flowers; it was a good garden plant. In every garden a dry summer thins out the ranks of lobelias, and East Lambrook lost many named varieties when they had insufficient shade and not enough water at the root. *Aconitum napellus*, the monkshood, is similar in form and problems. Spark's Variety in dark, deep blue was a useful plant flowering in July; *napellus* Bicolor in navy and white, and the autumn-flowering bright blue *A.fischeri* and rich blue *A.wilsoni* were valuable for their colour at a time when blue is scarce. She never felt she could do justice to *A. napellus* Bressingham Spire because with its solid spikes of intense violet it was a plant which did not need any company. The lemon-flowered *Aconitum lycoctonum (Vulparia)*, the wolfbane, suited her plantings by wandering through a low shrub, its angular flower spikes finding their own support.

Some of the species Michaelmas daisies produce their small flowers in the shade. A few all-purpose favourites were the species *Aster diffusus (lateriflorus)* Horizontalis, and the *A. ericoides* hybrids like Blue Star, Mrs G.N. Launder, Delight and White Heather; the pale rosy-lilac Hon Vicary Gibbs and Golden Spray offered good colour contrasts.

The *cordifolius* asters also flower in shade and the garden grew old ones like Photograph and Ideal, with Silver Spray, Elegans and Sweet Lavender, which stood in graceful clumps. Margery never cluttered them with other plants of the same height. *Aster turbinellus* Lewis Jones in French blue and the bushier *tradescantii* in white would flower until the frosts. The only tall aster found to be happy in shade was The Empress with its crimson centres and short lavender rays the size of a sixpence; Margery marvelled at the splendid show it made every year.

TREES AND SHRUBS FOR SHADE

One of the problems of shade gardening is the need for the permanent effect offered by shrubs. Though it is untrue that no evergreen
will grow in shade, the desire for flowers throughout the year led to
interesting experiments with shrubs in difficult places. It is well known
that hamamelis will survive in the sun, but tolerate more lime in the
shade, particularly out of the wind, and eventually she grew *Hamamelis
mollis, mollis* Brevipetala in deep gold and the lemon-flowered *H.
japonica* Zuccariniana. Her delight in extending Eleanour Sinclair
Rohde's green-into-gold theme stopped her from planting *Hamamelis
x intermedia* Ruby Glow, a dusky red, with red leaves in the autumn.

The species hydrangeas grow much better out of the wind and in the
shade. Margery frequently recounted seeing two groups of *Hydrangea
villosa* at Dartington Hall, Devon, where the one in shelter far outgrew
the other, but each had equal shade. *Hydrangea sargentiana* should re-
ceive similar treatment. The paler shades of *hortensis* do not demand
shade; the deeper colours are usually more tender. In the churchyard
at St Just-in-Roseland, Cornwall, Margery enjoyed the exotic use of
Hydrangea hortensis in a range of blue she could not hope to match on
her alkaline soil. All the lacecap hydrangeas do well in shade, particularly *H. serrata* Grayswood, changing from blue flowers to pink, then
crimson as it aged, with crimson leaves. *Hydrangea involucrata* in blue
or lilac was planted in the rock garden, and the double-flowering *H.
involucrata* Hortensis Margery thought was one of the most beautiful
shrubs she had ever grown.

Corylopsis pauciflora with pale primrose-coloured, cowslip-scented
flowers in March, was a borderline shrub for East Lambrook: it needed
neutral soil with shade and protection from wind and frost to succeed,
but when its heart-shaped leaves turned gold in autumn Margery considered the effort worthwhile.

Epigaea repens is a low-growing mat-forming shrub for moist, lime-
free peaty soil and deep shade; its pink flowers glow in the spring. Her
attempts to grow it, and *Epigaea asiatica* failed: the alkalinity of East
Lambrook soil excluded many highly suitable species. Two successes that
might not have been expected were pernettyas and *Skimmia japonica* –

skimmias were grown with great success, confounding every expert.

Japanese maples were used but Margery did not like their form and their need of neutral soil was no help. She went to immense lengths to please her cassiopes: shade, moisture, peat, no lime, nothing was too much trouble for this small shrub – though some of the smaller azaleas and rhododendrons could have provided more colour in this situation.

Amelanchier canadensis, snowy mespilus, grew in light shade at East Lambrook – a tree of many talents. In April its snow-white flowers shine among its coppery leaves, followed by crimson berries in July, a great treat for the birds; in autumn the leaves are a strange scarlet and in winter the twigs give a purple effect. *Stranvaesia davidiana* contributed its bronzy-red foliage and hawthorn flowers in June, and in autumn scarlet berries with scarlet foliage.

Viburnums were very good at East Lambrook with *V. foetens* and its pink fragrant flowers at the top of the list for shade. *Viburnum grandiflorum* was not so easy to grow; *V.fragrans* lived up to its name. Margery enjoyed the guelder rose *Viburnum opulus*, but in 1962 decided that if she ever started another garden she would plant *V.opulus* Xanthocarpum with yellow berries, which makes a smaller tree. She grew both *burkwoodii* and *carlesii* in shade, but the best of the viburnums for a shaded site was *plicatum tomentosum*, with dark leaves turning crimson in autumn and flowers in large creamy-white snowballs.

The ground-cover *Viburnum davidii* with its dense evergreen leaves offered turquoise October berries which the birds left alone – that made the trouble of planting male and female plants together worthwhile. The blue berries of *Symplocos crataegoides (paniculata)* are more brilliant, but in the Savill Gardens they were caged when ripening!

· *Leycesteria formosa* (pheasant berry) was planted for the blue-green foliage of its numerous seedlings, which found a ready home in the nursery. Its graceful arching stems dripped with white flowers and claret bracts, and its smooth green bark glowed in winter, when colour is important. Similarly *Lavatera olbia* was generous with its seedlings, and had large rose-pink flowers at every leaf axil continuously until early winter. In early spring its 6ft stems were dead and were cut to the ground, but regrowth was prompt.

Along the top path, light shade from *Acer pennsylvanicum* and the lonicera hedge
was sufficient to protect the cyclamen and the hellebores

Wise use of the bark colour of shrubs brought winter colour to the gardens. The dogwoods were valuable in this respect, and they tolerated shade. *Cornus alba* Spaethii, with red stems and leaves striped with gold, was a particular success. *Cornus alba* Westonbirt had bright red stems in winter with the added bonus of green leaves and small pale blue berries.

Daphnes grew well at East Lambrook; they like a cool soil, with plenty of humus and not too dry. The native *Daphne laureola* will grow in any soil, and provide ample seedlings on the heaviest clay; its tough dark evergreen leaves were complemented by small green scented flowers. *Daphne mezereum* and Daphne Somerset *(D. x burkwoodii)* grew well under cover, and *D. mezereum* Alba with the larger Grandiflora Alba, were good for brightening a dull corner in early spring. The yellowish-green leaves of *D. pontica* show up well in shade, where its creamy-green scented flowers are freely produced. *Daphne blagayana* does well if left alone to produce its long-stemmed scented cream flowers. The accepted method of propagation is to put stones over a low branch to make it root, but it is not a good idea to do so too frequently: the plant soon shows its resentment – as will *D. cneorum*. The gold picoteed leaf-edge of the variegated form is attractive, as is the scent of the flowers. A good cultivar that was difficult to establish was *Daphne cneorum* Eximea; Margery assumed that for some reason the greensand of her soil did not suit the small plants brought by a friend from a lime-free garden near Birmingham.

Daphnes do best if moved when young. *Daphne collina* and *D. tangutica* were planted in choice shady spots. When a plant of *retusa* grew slowly over a path, Margery decided that she did not dare to transplant the daphne, so moved the path. Some years previously a plant of *D. genkwa* on its own roots had grown out of the shade and into the sun; instead of planting more shade, she moved the daphne and lost it. She decided after many attempts at establishing *Daphne arbuscula* that once she had it settled successfully she would never move it even if the garden had to be reconstructed around it.

An uncommon and attractive shrub called *Neillia longiracemosa (thibetica)*, with pink flowers like a spirea in May and June, grew happily in shade in company with the bladder senna, *Colutea arborescens*, whose yellow flowers and popping seed-pods are enjoyed by children. In the sun this shrub will grow up to 12ft, but in shade it worked hard

to achieve 6ft; nor did it flower as freely under the weeping willow.

Mahonias, surprisingly, were not widely grown in the 1960s. Margery realised the merits of *Mahonia japonica* for every month of the year; in winter the sprays of primrose-coloured flowers scented like lily-of-the valley were displayed against dark, prickly evergreen foliage which turned russet in autumn. It grows best in cool peaty soil in shade, being kept low by pruning after flowering – making a cut at the rough thickening about 6in below where the flower sprays emerge, to encourage new growth to break. *Mahonia lomariifolia* was at the edge of its hardy range at East Lambrook. It made a good upright shrub in shade with its stiff leaves and long straight spikes of unscented flowers of deep yellow, but to be well displayed needed softer looser plants around it. *Mahonia aquifolium* was a suitable shape but both it and the variety Undulata wandered too much; they were better for underplanting trees in light woodland. *Mahonia nervosa* liked a similar environment with light soil, but it was slow to establish. It made good ground cover, with copper-coloured glossy leaves and primrose-coloured flowers, and was the best companion for *M. lomariifolia*.

Euonymus europaeus, our native spindleberry of hedges and spinneys, was grown for its delicate autumn colour and brilliant berries of old rose. In some conspicuous places in the garden the form Red Cascade had such a good shape it was surrounded with low-growing plants, so that the arching boughs with large rosy-red fruits could be enjoyed; for pollination she used *E. hamiltonianus* with soft pink fruits and a similar graceful form. Two other spindles, *E. planipes (sachaliensis)* and *E. alatus*, added their coloured berries to the autumn display.

Olearia gunniana (phlogopappa), the Tasmanian daisy bush, is marginally hardy away from the coast, and a severe winter would kill it at East Lambrook. Margery was constantly amused by being complimented on having white Michaelmas daisies in June – much as Mrs Clive Ponsonby Fane once had her 'dandelions' admired.

Spiraeas grow well in shade. *Spiraea arguta* (bridal wreath) has arching sprays of white flowers in April; Anthony Waterer was found a better form, with its flat heads of crimson flowers and young leaves of pink and cream. *Spiraea prunifolia* Plena has rounded shiny foliage which turns crimson in October, with pearl-like flowers in May, somewhat later than the small star-like flowers of *thunbergii*, whose light green leaves stayed fresh until November, and started again in January.

Some of the dwarfer deutzias also flourish in the shade. A good white is *Deutzia x rosea* Campanulata; *elegantissima* is very graceful with rose-pink flowers, and *kalmiiflora* has large pink and white flowers in clusters over the whole bush. *Buplerum fruticosum* with yellowy-green flowers was happy under trees in company with forsythia and *Cotoneaster simonsii* and *bullata*. Aucubas flourished; both green and spotted have good scarlet berries for flower arrangers when stripped of their leaves. *Danae racemosa*, Alexandrian laurel, was an excellent evergreen shrub for underplanting, and ruscus, butcher's broom, tolerates deep dry shade: Treseder's Variety was the best form grown, because being hermaphrodite it has many red berries in the winter. Margery did not dislike privet, but felt it needed correct placing to avoid its bad reputation. *Ligustrum compactum*, *delavayanum* and *japonicum*, with the gold and silver variegated forms of *ovalifolium*, make a good contrast as specimens or trained against a wall.

Some of the dwarf conifers can help transform a mixed shady border or rock garden if not overlaid by other plants, because their form and texture add distinction to the plantings. She constantly experimented with heathers and daboecias in the shade, but the alkalinity of the soil prevented a wide range of them being grown. The *Erica carnea* group with their winter-flowering habit and tolerance of lime were the most successful, and she admired their colour range.

SHADY WALLS NEED COVERING

Margery was proud of the way she clothed any available walls – her reaction during the Malthouse fire when her first thought was to save the climbing plants and forget the furniture indoors was an example. Until she gardened seriously the use of decorative climbers had been largely confined to south and west walls; north and east walls were frequently left for jasmines and ivies. To her eye for a good plant she added a willingness to try it in new situations. For example by adding peat and sequestrene to the soil under a north wall she grew both japonica and williamsii camellias, particularly J.C. Williams and the deeper pink Mary Christian.

The climbing *Hydrangea petiolaris* with its large corymbs of creamy-white flowers was another splendid shady-wall plant, though deciduous;

Looking west in the front garden. Clematis, roses and hydrangeas clothed and softened the walls

she found it freer-flowering than the evergreen *Hydrangea integerrima (serratifolia)*. The closely allied *Schizophragma hydrangeoides*, with one showy bract-like sepal to each cream flower, made a good companion to the golden-flowered winter jasmine, *J. nudiflorum*, which flowers from November until April. *Jasminum officinale*, with its dark green foliage lightened by scented stars of white in June, carrying on until the end of autumn, was equally good. Margery found the gold and silver variegations of this too restrained in growth for her exuberant gardening style while the pink-flushed flowers of *J. officinale* Grandiflorum (Affine) were too few for the green sprays.

Akebia quinata is practically evergreen, and its slender habit makes it a good plant to grow up others on a north wall. It has scented chocolate-purple flowers, male and female on the same plant, five-lobed leaves and in suitable seasons 3in purple fruits; these split open to show black seeds in a downy white pulp. Its greatest

assets are its twining habit, and handsome foliage. Aristolochias have these attributes too, with foliage in greenish-yellow and purple-brown. *Aristolochia macrophylla*, Dutchman's pipe, was the form grown, and she recommended the smaller *tomentosa* to her friends. The twining *Mutisia retusa* with holly leaves and pink daisy flowers needed constant support and ample moisture to grow 8ft high against a north wall, higher indeed than the everlasting pea *Lathyrus latifolius* ever reached in the shade at East Lambrook. The varieties White Pearl, Pink Beauty and Red Pearl grew in the shade.

Several honeysuckles grew on north-facing walls, usually the large-flowered woodland type which suffered from greenfly if planted in the sun. Unscented with rich yellow flowers veined with red, *Lonicera tellmanniana* was excellent, as were the early and late Dutch honeysuckles, *Lonicera periclymenum* Belgica and Serotina respectively. *Lonicera caprifolium* is scented, with pink-budded cream flowers and orange berries, a good companion for the shrubbier, longer-flowering *grata (americana)*, with sprays of pink and green flowers over several months. *Lonicera japonica* Halliana flowers later until the frosts and can be reduced in size in the spring.

Some clematis cultivars are suitable for shade. *Clematis tangutica* and *C.orientalis* are frequently confused – they have similar orange lantern flowers, and both will grow in shade. *Tangutica* flowers earlier and its silky seed heads last well into winter, like old man's beard. *Clematis rehderana* grew with *tangutica* on the same shady wall, its small bunches of primrose-coloured flowers, scented like cowslips, mixing with the yellow and silver of *tangutica*. Not quite so successful at East Lambrook was *Clematis calycina (cirrhosa* var. *balearica)*, with ferny evergreen foliage and small greenish-ivory flowers freckled inside with maroon.

Solanum jasminoides needs a warm wall, but *Solanum crispum* will grow anywhere. The Glasnevin form grew on a shady east wall where its mauve potato-flowers burnished with gold centres coloured summer and autumn. *Tropaeolum speciosum* needs a north wall and will then climb to the sun to flower, but if the sun cannot be found it will flower in the shade. Margery once saw it flowering and making its blue berries against a tall tree in complete shade. *Berberidopsis corallina*, the coral plant of Chile, is a good evergreen climber with dark leaves and hanging coral flowers that must be grown in shade.

Roses can be successful against a shady wall. Mme Alfred Carrière is

a classic example, growing and flowering prodigiously, as will Albèric Barbier. Mermaid is slow to start, but will grow in sun or shade, and lives longer as a small plant on its own roots rather than budded. The China rose, *Rosa chinensis*, grown in shade blooms most of the year: East Lambrook had the old pink monthly rose, *R. chinensis* Old Blush and Fellemberg in rose-crimson; Hermosa in silvery-pink was next to *Garrya elliptica* on a north wall. The green rose, *Rosa* Viridiflora, with its maroon centre, flowered under a north hedge. *Rosa filipes* Kiftsgate, the vigorous climber from China, flowered happily in shade.

Ivies, of course, do not mind how much shade there is; it is surprising that with her interest in every possible ivy cultivar for ground cover, she did not take one large wall and arrange their growth by size and colour. The semi-double red *Cydonia (Chaenomeles) superba* Simonii, and the white *C. japonica* Alba grew in dark corners, with the low-growing *Cydonia lagenaria (speciosa)* Moerloosei in apple-blossom pink on low white walls. Escallonias, pyracanthas and cotoneasters in variety were used to cover almost every shady area.

She liked yellow and white for shady walls, and a favourite combination was *Forsythia suspensa* on an east wall with *Viburnum tomentosum plicatum* Grandiflorum to extend the flowering period. Laburnums, rosemaries and deutzias had considerable success in semi-shady positions. For permanent plantings she preferred to grow the glossy-leaved shrubs, such as *Garrya elliptica*, *Fatsia japonica* and *Mahonia aquifolium*, which flowers when *Mahonia japonica* finishes; or with the early-flowering white *Osmanthus delavayi*, an excellent shrub for a shady spot. If asked for a snap judgement on a shrub to plant in shade, she would usually reply *Kerria japonica* (Jew's mallow) – if this shrub were difficult everyone would want to grow its orange or yellow, single or double flowers.

GOLD AND SILVER FOR SHADE

To combine gold and silver in a garden was not unusual in 1880, but by 1950 it had ceased to be considered attractive. To Margery's credit she saw its potential for a dull shady spot. As most of the best gold and silver leaved plants prefer to grow in the sun, the idea required study and hard work in successful propagation. Among the golden-leaved plants she used were *Lamium maculatum* and Bowles' golden grass, *Milium*

effusum Aureum. The short-lived *Veronica teucrium* Trehane usually survived in the shade of a taller plant or shrub. *Origanum vulgare* Aureum was one of the most successful golden plants in the shade, privet *Ligustrum ovalifolium* Aureum the most successful golden-leaved shrub; the golden variegated forms of eleagnus were in Margery's opinion the most refined leaf form. Interestingly, she once lost the golden form of the philadelphus, *coronarius* Aureus by giving it too much exposure to strong midday light.

Silver-foliaged plants like hot dry positions in poor soil, but by accident a seedling of *Senecio cineraria* White Diamond was planted in shade, and Margery was delighted to find it grew as well as any in the sun. So did *Santolina neapolitana*, and the neater *Santolina incana*. Artemesia proved to be less insistent on sun than some silver plants and kept their colour, but the taller forms became leggy and drawn. *Artemesia stelleriana* and *ludoviciana* kept their appearance, but *absinthium*, and its improved form Lambrook Silver, were the most satisfactory – needing a similar amount of sunlight to *Helichrysum angustifolium (serotinum)*, and the bushy *Helichrysum triliniatum (splendidum)*. Margery experimented with this in company with *Anaphalis triplinervis* and the taller *margaritacea*, using tough *Senecio greyi* under the trees if the soil was poor and dry.

It is but a short way from a gold and silver garden in the shade to a variegated garden and she took this direction, realising the uses of variegated leaves in her quest to achieve colour in the garden throughout the year. Those that will grow in the shade with clay and lime are limited, however, and the usual trials-and-errors threw out some interesting cultivars. Her rule originally was golden variegation for sun and silver for shade, but the success of golden ivies, such as *Hedera helix* Buttercup, or golden-variegated *Iris pallida* soon turned this on its head. The variegated crown imperial, which does better in half-shade than sun, she had coveted since seeing it at Myddleton House, Enfield.

By extending this thought she found all the variegated grasses doing just as well in shade as sun – Constance Spry advocated many of those in the garden. The handsome striped forms of *Miscanthus sinensis* were frequently used in contrast with *Miscanthus sinensis* Zebrinus with horizontal golden bands all the way up the stems. Gardener's garters (*Phalaris arundinacea* Picta) is easy in shade, and was planted in with purple-leaved shrubs – the purple filbert *Corylus maxima* Atropurpurea,

Pollarded willows dominated the ditch garden in early spring

Berberis thunbergii Atropurpurea, or purple rhus. She then cut it early
to make a carpet of pale green and white, unless she needed the length
of pale white leaves. The dwarf bulbous-rooted *Arrhenatherum elatius*
Bulbosum Variegatum was better in the shade. Taller variegated grasses
and rushes she always considered magnificent, and another favourite
planting was to put mounds of variegated foliage under shrubs. The
variegated apple mint *Mentha rotundifolia* Variegata gave the best contrast, because the deeper the shade the whiter it is; the golden-variegated
'ginger mint' *gentilis* Aurea, tended to run but was equally successful.
Margery particularly liked the speckled leaves of variegated horehound
Marrubium vulgare.

In those days *Lamium galeobdolon* Variegatum (creeping yellow
archangel), with its leaves of silver and grey-green, was still an unusual
plant. Margery realised its invasive potential and used it to transform the
dark green of ivy leaves by way of competition. Like its relative *Lamium
maculatum* it can grow very strongly in difficult terrain. Periwinkles, too
were liked, and the variegated forms obligingly lightened dark shady
corners. Variegated bugle in green and pink was another plant used
for shade, with *Nepeta hederacea* Variegata, and *Pachysandra terminalis*

Variegata. Despite the large numbers of geraniums Margery grew, she only had two variegated forms – *Geranium macrorrhizum*, more cream than green, and *punctatum* which actually seeded itself in the garden.

The best of the variegated iris was thought to be *foetidissima* Variegata. It was at its most brilliant in winter, and never whiter than in deep shade. *Iris japonica* needs mild weather and a sheltered position; *pseudacorus* turns green at the end of summer, while *laevigata* waits for the spring to make its leaves: these were all silver and do best in shade. Only *pallida* was gold and was definitely a plant for shade.

She found the most useful variegated plants were evergreens, and was always keen to include *Scrophularia aquatica* Variegata and symphytums in her plantings. The variegated strawberry kept its leaves, as did rue, which she found was best cut back in April; even though early cuttings lose their variegation they usually grow back into colour.

The variegated honesty *Lunaria annua* Variegata with its flowers of royal purple, striped with white, was one of her best plants for shade. The plain purple cultivars needed taking out, because eventually they would take the planting over. Seed of the variegated nasturtium was easily obtainable and always grew true.

Variegated sedums were some of her most spectacular variegated plants, and several forms were sold from the nursery: *Sedum telephium* Roseo-Variegatum, and the ordinary *Sedum spectabile* Variegatum. The variegated form of *Veronica gentianoides* was good ground cover for the front of a shady border, like the golden London pride with its showy rosettes of green and gold.

Variegated Shrubs

These herbaceous plants were outnumbered by variegated shrubs. Margery grew euonymus in many varieties, as successfully as two forms of variegated box, which she clipped to combine with *Daphne odora* Aureomarginata and *Daphne cneorum* to provide a colourful low background. She was continually cherishing seedlings from variegated *Daphne mezereum*, but never succeeded in making them grow variegated. *Buddleia davidii* Royal Red was probably her favourite variegated shrub, its flowers the richest of all the buddleias, with striking cream and green leaves. It grew well in the shade, but was more effective in

the sun, attracting butterflies. The variegated poplar, *Populus candicans* Aurora, with its leaves of pink and cream, tolerated shade but needed winter pruning to get the best colour from its young leaves.

The gold and silver hollies, with broad or narrow leaves, all did well in shade. The hedgehog holly *Ilex acquifolium* Ferox, with its slow-growing prickly leaves was an excellent choice for a restricted area in the garden – in both silver and gold forms, though the silver (Ferox Argentea) remained her favourite choice, with its brightly margined prickles.

Innocence, the variegated philadelphus, with leaves marked with deep cream, must be grown in shade. It was planted alongside what she considered one of the neatest and most attractive of variegated shrubs, *Rhamnus alternus variegata*, evergreen with silver-grey and white foliage. Its only fault was its distress in hard winters, which made it slow-growing. It eventually reached 6ft and was considered as of the same hardiness as *Fuchsia magellanica*.

The cornus family with variegated leaves were more tolerant of the limy soil than such types as *Cornus kousa*. Margery's collection of variegated dogwoods which grew successfully in the shade included *Cornus alba* Sibirica Variegata with white markings on leaves of grey-green. Cornus *alba* Spaethii had more gold in its leaves and stems, making it a dual-purpose plant. *C. mas* Variegata she described as triple-purpose, for as well as having silver-variegated leaves all summer, spidery flowers on the stems in February and March gave way to red cherry-like fruit.

When variegation is tricolor, the effect is especially attractive growing over a wall or on a bank. The graceful, spreading *Fuchsia magellanica* Versicolor is smaller than some fuchsias and its leaves of silver touched with pink made it a frequently used plant at East Lambrook; *magellanica* Riccartonii is a larger plant, and the pinker leaves gave a crimson effect in the distance. Margery grew them with the tricolor St John's wort, *Hypericum x moseranum*, under trees. The hypericum has a low spreading habit which was also good under shrubs or tall perennials as a ground cover of white, pink and green shading to crimson on the edges. *Polygonum cuspidatum* is a strong-growing plant and invasive, but the leaves of crimson, cream and green make it startling.

On a north wall, *Jasminum officinale*, variegated in white, tinged with pink and touched with gold, was one of the most effective climbers planted. It was greatly preferred to *Jasminum nudiflorum* Aureo Variegata, where there was not enough gold to make the leaf look variegated.

Lonicera japonica Aureoreticulata, with its dull green leaves netted with fine gold lines, was in her view a more suitable companion, particularly when the leaves were mottled pink in summer. These were the safest of her variegated shrubs and climbers in the shade.

No one before had so fully explored how many different plants could be grown in the shade. In the course of her experiments Margery focused on the uses of four species of plant which effectively changed the face of English plantsmanship to this day: her work with hellebores has been discussed earlier, and her work with bergenias, hostas, and euphorbias too has had a lasting effect on gardening design. It was not at the outset her intention to change the plants of our gardens – in fact quite the contrary. As many people remarked about Margery, her eye for a good plant was unfailing, and when she discovered a species new to her she tried every available cultivar. Only the fact that she is remembered by the public for her work with cottage-garden flowers has obscured her lasting reputation as an originator of a newer, more interesting style of gardening in shade.

Rosa Nevada with *Euphorbia* Lambrook Gold
The statue that was stolen, with *Campanula muralis*

(page 120) Polemonium and *Gladiolus byzantinus*

10

Stream and Woodland

One of the regrets at East Lambrook was that the ditch garden was not large enough for all the plants for damp shade Margery wished to grow. Her beloved primroses and violets needed most of the space. Such shade plants as gunneras and rodgersia had to be strictly controlled; they need a large area and lose their attraction if crowded in with other plants.

Among plants tried in rotation was the umbrella plant *Peltiphyllum peltatum*, lately called *Saxifraga peltata*; its creeping rhizomes will bind the damp soil on the edge of a bank or pool. Early in spring the bare red stems open to wide heads of pink starry flowers, and after these are over then the leaves appear.

Lysichitum (bog arum), which is similar to the skunk cabbage, needs very damp soil right at the edge of a running stream, and although usually planted in sun it will succeed in shade. It also needs space for the large leaves. Margery found *Lysichitum americanum* the most dramatic of the family. The yellow flowers like giant arums came through the soil in early spring, to be followed by giant green leaves, which needed a green background or at most the company of small white flowers. She disliked it grown with *Primula rosea* as is frequently done, preferring *Lysichitum camshatcense* with its pure white flowers and smaller, luminous not glossy, grey-green leaves.

Ligularia clivorum (dentata) is another strongly individual plant, with large leathery dark green leaves of a heart shape, through which emerge vivid orange daisies on stout stems. The variety Othello with leaves and stems of dark purple gave a rich effect; the smaller Desdemona, with red-green leaves lined with crimson faded to a metallic green. Most of these senecios, renamed ligularia, prefer sunshine, but the Polish *Ligularia przewalskii* was grown in damp shade; a slender plant with tapering spines of tiny yellow flowers and deep-cut foliage, it paid for its space in late summer.

Senecio tanguticus was a handsome plant eliminated eventually because of its wandering habit, but a small piece was left in a dry position and

delighted all with its controlled growth. The handsome foliage and triangular spikes of yellow flowers tempered with green were followed by fluffy silken seed-heads and silver bracts for indoor decoration. *Senecio smithii* from the Falkland Isles is a fleshy plant, with thick dark leaves and flowers of short-rayed white daisies on thick stems. Planted in a ditch under a north wall it looked comfortable, but had not the fascination of *Senecio pulcher*. This is a plant out of the ordinary, with long dark leaves covered with white hairs and notched at the edges, and solid rosy-pink flowers. Its late flowering habit meant it needed protection if grown in exposed places. In a fairly damp narrow bed under an east-facing wall it gave complete satisfaction.

Astilbes will grow in an ordinary flower bed, but are better in moist shade; Margery felt that gardeners did not make enough use of them. By the water they complement, by contrast, the plants with big solid leaves. Some have bronze leaves in the spring, others are mahogany-coloured through the season. At East Lambrook they were never cut down until the new growth appeared in the spring because the stems and seed-heads stay a warm cigar-brown throughout the winter. At the time when Margery was gardening, a new variety of astilbe was introduced every year. It was not in her nature to turn out a satisfactory old variety for the sake of a new one unless a complete colour break occurred, as in the case of Red Sentinel. The varieties grown were Garnet, Fanal, Rose, the crimson, bronze-foliaged William Reeves, pink Betsy Cuperus and Apple Blossom, white Avalanche and Irrlicht, creamy-white King Albert, salmon Vesuvius and lilac-purple Amethyst. The dumpy *Astilbe chinensis* Pumila was planted in damp shade, because it made excellent ground cover and its foot-high flower spikes in mauve-pink are sturdy if not striking. The pale pink Perkeo did not grow as well as the type, but the white *Astilbe simplicifolia* with fine-cut deep-coloured foliage, and its taller cousin Atrorosea in deep pink, with the bronze leaves and pink flowers of Bronze Elegance, filled the space.

Some of the filipendulas, which are mostly slightly taller than the astilbes, made such good ground cover for damp shade that she could not ignore them. The tall *Filipendula purpurea* with leafy stems and flat heads of bright pink flowers was a tough plant for a difficult position; *hexapetala* Flore Pleno with pale pink buds and double cream flowers was good ground cover in a drier position. The double meadow sweet,

Filipendula ulmaria Flore Pleno, its golden form and the one with variegated foliage, were excellent plants for damp shade, where they showed up well.

A plant that found popular acclaim was Margery's beloved *Ranunculus aconitifolius* Flore Pleno, the old 'fair maids of France'. It has handsome cut green leaves and small white button flowers on branching stems. Popular in Stuart times, this plant had fallen out of general cultivation and by describing it in her lectures she re-established it as the truly good cottage-garden plant it is. After flowering it disappears below ground; it can be increased by dividing its claw-like roots. Only at Hidcote did she ever see its single form: taller and thinner, it needed massing for a telling display.

The double buttercups grew in shade. Her favourite was *Ranunculus carpaticus* with large glistening yellow flowers that had green centres. She also grew the smaller runner, *speciosus plenus*, and the lovely double-flowering meadow buttercup *Ranunculus acris* Fore Pleno. Similar conditions suited the allied trollius. Margery had great affection for the early *Trollius europaeus* with pale primrose flowers on 18in stems. The hybrid Byrne's Giant was lemon yellow and others grew deeper in colour until they reached the rich Orange Queen. She never mastered the pale cream Alabaster, delicate in colour and constitution.

Lysimachia ephemerum reminded her of a kind old lady in a grey dress who showed up the colours of others nearby; the small pale flowers were on sufficiently long and graceful spikes to be considered a useful plant for damp shade. *L. clethroides* had white flowers shaped like a shepherd's crook; it was usually planted against a wall or taller shrubs at East Lambrook, so all the crooks faced the same way. It spread by suckering but was less invasive than the yellow-flowered *Lysimachia punctata* which even in a dry position would invade the neighbours.

From country walks Margery became attracted to the ordinary purple loosestrife *Lythrum salicaria*; she grew a wide range of seedlings from the named varieties in her shady ditch garden, from rose-red to pink and purple. *Lythrum virgatum* was of different growth, with many spikes of small bright pink flowers; the usually grown variety Rose Queen was not as pleasing as the purple loosestrife.

ARCHITECTURAL LEAVES FOR DAMP SHADE

Occasionally she felt a lack of architectural leaves for damp shade, and used iris species to attract the eye from a distance with their form. *Iris ochroleuca* was tallest, a good 4ft, with white flowers and yellow falls; Ochraurea had yellow flowers with deeper yellow markings. The surprise was that at East Lambrook *Iris sibirica* was grown in shade in a wide colour range, from the pale blue-grey of the type to the china blue of Perry's Blue and the Oxford blue of Mrs Saunders. Violet was provided by Caesar and Emperor, while Eric the Red was the reddest. Snow Queen showed up well in a damp dark corner, and was most widely planted as the focal point of the grouping.

Iris laevigata likes to grow near if not actually in the water. Margery much admired a large planting of the variegated form in a pond under a tree in a friend's garden. The old-rose *Iris laevigata* Rose Queen was an unusual colour, with an attractive white form; this iris does not like lime and did not increase at East Lambrook. It tended to be overshadowed by *Iris setosa* in deep blue and crimson and the common yellow flag, *I. pseudacorus*. The primrose-coloured form and the variegated-leafed one for spring leaf colour were planted with the white chrysanthemum Moon Daisy and the Cambridge-blue flowers of *Salvia uliginosa*.

Phormiums or the New Zealand flaxes have a strong architectural habit which makes them most decorative in English gardens; but after a run of mild winters, when they have become popular, along comes a cold winter and they die – giving everyone who recommends them a bad name. Margery noted that in the winter of 1961–2 only those growing under trees survived. They can be grown from seed, or split into sections with a sharp spade and a discerning eye for plenty of root. *Phormium tenax* in grey-green was good, with its broad 6ft leaves, but the variegated forms *P. tenax Variegatum*, striped creamy-yellow, and *tenax* Veitchii with a broad golden stripe up the centre of each leaf, contrasted well with the crimson-purple sheen of Purpureum, particularly during the winter when the light came straight at them. The smallest of the range available at this time was *tenax* Alpinum.

PRIMULAS

Primula species grew in damp shade at East Lambrook in every colour but blue. There was no blue candelabra primula, although some of the lilac and lavender shades of the drumstick *Primula denticulata* approached it. *P. denticulata cachemiriana* has smaller leaves of grey-green and dainty dark-eyed, slaty-mauve flowers. The white and ruby-red forms of *denticulata* were generally preferred to this, and the stock increased by seed and root cuttings – lifting a plant out of the ground, transplanting it and letting the roots left behind do the propagation.

Primula japonica suited East Lambrook. The plant carried a generous air about it, even though the magenta-red of the type did not suit all tastes. She preferred the named Millar's Crimson, Postford White and Rowallane Rose, though maintaining a stock proved difficult. The stems of *Primula pulverulenta* are thickly powdered and the type was a purplish-red; the Bartley strain in pink and pale salmon were also planted. There were two strains of candelabra primula, the Lissadel hybrids in shades of yellow, apricot, flame and salmon-pink, and the Asthore hybrids in the mauve and purple colours from *Primula bulleyana*. Primula *beesiana* had crimson scented flowers, and *Primula burmanica* had yellow eyes in the reddish-purple flowers.

Primula florindae (giant Himalayan cowslip) is the tallest of the yellow primulas and also the most robust. It flowers late and is strongly scented; its broad heart-shaped leaves were a further reason to grow it in every suitable situation. The golden-yellow *helodoxa* was more difficult to please, and Margery was always unhappy when a difficult plant defeated her. *Primula prolifera*, despite the silver sheen on the leaves and the clear cool yellow of the flowers, was not sufficient compensation. She settled eventually with the creamier shades of the pale *chionantha* with its pleasant scent, and the nodding fingered flowers of the Himalayan cowslip, *Primula sikkimensis*. These cream colours were mixed with the stronger burnt orange of *bulleyana*, a colour blend she enjoyed. *Primula vialii*, with violet flowers and scarlet calyces which make it look like a little red-hot poker, was no easier for her than any other gardener. The carmine pink of *Primula rosea* was set against a green background, with

no yellow or orange near; then all could enjoy the sealing-wax red of its buds and its bronze-tinged leaves.

She found the *petiolares* primulas difficult as they needed a damp sunless position, with the soil drawn up around their crowns and moist air. *Bhutanica* and *gracilipes* lasted for a season or two and eventually failed, but the *pubescens* primulas like the rich lavender Mrs Jill Wilson and the rare white Alba grew well in the shade in stone troughs.

Primroses were not usually planted in the rockery, two exceptions being the deep ivory Lady Greer and the small brick-red E.R. Janes; but the rockery was preferred for the farinosae primulas like the small rose-pink *clarkei* where she could control the line, with varieties like the lilac-flowered, powdered-leaved *farinosa*, and *frondosa* with a distinct yellow eye to its lilac flowers. *Primula rosea* needed more moisture than was available here.

A favourable plant suitable for damp shade, but occupying more space in the garden than Margery felt should be allowed was *Cardamine pratensis* Flore Pleno, the double-flowering version of the lady's smock; others were the marsh marigolds, like the double *Caltha palustris* Flore Pleno, mixed with the creamy-white and the bright gold of the single forms. Pride of place was reserved for the hose-in-hose musk *Mimulus luteus duplex* in yellow and bronze. Other mimulus, such as *cardinalis* in shades of red and yellow, were grown, and the A.T. Johnson form with red blotches on the petals. *Cupreus* Red Emperor and Whitecroft Scarlet were quite dwarf with the pointed hairy leaves of the rose-pink *Mimulus lewisii* acting as a contrast to the glossy leaves of the others. All these single forms seemed to slip away into the willows and bamboos, but the hose-in-hose musk was given to special garden visitors.

WILLOWS AND BAMBOOS

Willows and bamboos were not collected, for variety's sake; she preferred to select species from collections elsewhere. There was not room for a large number of willows. The weeping willow *Salix alba* Vitellina Pendula, with its golden bark, the silver silken leaves of the small *Salix alba* Argentea and the twisted silhouette of *Salix matsudana*

Silver birches provided light shade along the top path

Tortuosa were three which grew as small trees in damp shade. A few bamboos were considered sufficiently non-rampant to be admitted to the garden, including *Arundinaria nitida* with slender black-purple canes and small dark leaves, *A. murieliae* with yellow stems and narrow leaves, *A. japonica* with stems of pale grey-green and dark glossy foliage, and *A. pumila*, which grows only 6ft high in glossy dark green. The lovely golden bamboo *Arundinaria auricoma (viridistriata)* needs a sunny situation to keep its colour; in one of the rockeries it provided shade for various silver-variegated smaller bamboos and other shade-loving plants. Among these were several that usually grow in sunshine, but they could be accommodated in shade with lime.

SPRING COLOUR IN DAMP SHADE

A rough guess was that more rock plants suitable for shade than for sun could be found on acid soil but on lime it needed more care. *Omphalodes cappadocica* has a long period of flower if given shade and moisture on the lower slopes of a rock garden. Equally blue is *Omphalodes verna*, but it is not such a neat and reliable plant; it was grown with its white form, because of their early-flowering habit. *Omphalodes luciliae* is difficult, but it succeeded with a strict diet of grit and no lime under a north wall: the challenge was considered well worthwhile for its blue-grey leaves and pale blue flowers. Two aquilegias that enjoy shade were grown, a deep blue and white, and Viridiflora. This plant is rarely sold, yet grows easily from a spring sowing where it is intended to grow; its green flowers made it a plant to treasure at East Lambrook.

Lathyrus vernus (everlasting pea) provided early spring colour in shady damp situations. The prettiest was *Lathyrus vernus* Albo Roseus in pink and white which associated well with the purple-blue of *vernus*, the brilliant blue *Lathyrus cyaneus* and its white form. These plants contrasted with arabis, with its rather heavy rosettes, covered by its mass of white flowers. The white form usually grew in crevices in walls, while the less rampant pink forms of *muralis* and *albida (caucasica)* Rosa Bella had shade in the rock garden itself. Her favourite was the double white with its strong columns of flowers like a stock. The dark olive-green of the leaves of perennial candytuft were a welcome contrast here as the flowers grew in mounting tiers of white. At the base of the planting 2in

Iberis saxatilis flowered by the 6in *I. sempervirens,* mounted overall by the 1ft *sempervirens* Snowflake.

When people said they could not grow daisies, Margery said it was because they were planted in full sun; daisies needed shade and moisture. Her original plantings of Dresden China were gradually superseded in the gaps of the paving by *Gentiana acaulis,* but she used daisies in the shade in the garden as well as in rockwork. She was sympathetic to a plant which had some varieties still as they were when Gerard and Parkinson wrote about them, and some so sophisticated they were on the verge of becoming Victorian florist flowers. She grew the pink Alice and white Robert in the rock garden with many of her collected forms with variegated foliage and small pale rose-tipped flowers; she was reluctant to add the hen-and-chickens daisy to this position, feeling its character more in keeping with the green garden.

Arenaria balearica was the most successful and the three varieties grown on the shady side of the rock garden; *montana* and *purpurascens* were decidedly difficult to keep without direct sunlight. All the androsaces were good plants for shade, reproducing themselves by sending down runners and making small rosettes followed by pale pink flowers; *sarmentosa* and *microphylla* were grown with equal success. The asperulas like shade, but they cannot tolerate winter rain, needing a pane of glass to protect them. Margery grew the varieties *gussonii, lilaciflora, caespitosa* and *subrosa.*

Hepaticas, in theory, had all the attributes of Margery's favourite plants. They had been grown since the Middle Ages because of their medicinal use for liver complaints; they enjoyed shade and the rooting medium East Lambrook garden could give them. But she never kept many clumps of the common varieties and the rare double red and blue she ignored, at a time when her contemporaries Mrs Emerson of Limavady and Mary McMurtrie of Balbithan in Scotland were growing them in some quantity. Margery grew the sky-blue February-flowering *transylvanica* and the *triloba x transylvanica* called Ballard's Variety, with the medium-blue Loddon Blue and the lilac-pink flowers of *lilacina.* The *triloba* varieties with their marbled foliage or early double flowers failed to excite her, perhaps because the flowers were less formal and the plant less easy to propagate than the double primrose.

PLANTS WITH IMPACT

The reason why Margery's gardening in the shade was so successful and widely copied was because she demonstrated that shade could be used to grow individual plants with immediate impact. She never consciously developed these plants as a theme, but in private conversation referred to them as personality plants; she said they would cover a range of indifferent planting, because their flowers were so striking that garden visitors would be pleased to see them well grown and not criticise her bad points too seriously.

The type of plant she had in mind was the veratrum, a plant of the Australian foothills, usually seen in its blackish-maroon flowering form. Two variants showed up better against a dark background, the yellowish-white *album* (false helleborine), and the green-flowered form, *viride* (Indian poke). The individual blossoms grow tightly against tall stems, with veined petals and prominent stamens. Originally they were planted in the ditch garden, but eventually the green flowers of *viride* were moved to the green garden, where with plenty of added humus they grew well in more exposed conditions. In the same planting was *Kirengeshoma palmata*, an unusual September-flowering plant from Japan, with both grace and distinction. Its large vine-like leaves are on black whippy stems, the flowers like pale yellow crystal shuttlecocks hovering above the plant. It was grown in a peat bed against a north wall, for it hates lime and needs moisture.

Fascicularia bicolor was another of her plants of distinction. She found it needed shade to give its best. Light blue anemone-like flowers nestled at the base of the slender spring leaves, which turn salmon-pink at flowering time to attract – in its native Chile – the humming-birds for pollination. *Morina longifolia* is a plant with equally unusual foliage: the long prickly leaves are like a thistle's, but when complemented by tall spikes of hooded white flowers the effect is memorable. As the florets age they turn from white to pink to crimson. To establish easily it needs planting when small, because the long taproot readily bleeds if damaged. The leaves and stems were never cut down, for the skeleton stems had great beauty in the winter garden.

Roscoea cautleoides gave a luxuriant, tropical effect in a shaded

sheltered corner, its large canna-like leaves with stems of mahogany and pale yellow flowering regularly and increasing well. *Roscoea lutea* had deeper yellow flowers with green leaves. Their close relatives the hedychiums (ginger lilies) did better in the light shade of taller perennials; given full sun they did not survive a hard winter. Margery got this idea after seeing *Hedychium densiflorum* growing away well from a sheltering shrub in a London garden after a hard winter.

One plant which has survived the rigours of East Lambrook to this day is the hardy begonia, *Begonia evansiana*, in pink and white. In the sunken Renaissance garden of the Villa Torrigana at Lucca in Tuscany, this plant blooms to perfection in September and October, receiving regular dousings from the water jokes – a feature there. Margery realised this and grew them for autumn colour in the ditch garden, in company with the rare and elegant Cambridgeshire parsley *Selinum carvifolia*. A relative of our roadside Queen Anne's lace, 4 to 5ft high, it had broad fernlike leaves and large flat heads of white flowers. Pink forms of both these were planted and mixed effectively, making one of her most admired groupings. Rhubarb, she said, was worth growing in shade for its handsome leaves and elegant flowers, because the pink-flowered *Rheum palmatum* was so colourful; its huge leaves are lined with red and when the 4ft high spikes of raspberry-pink flowers rise over the leaves it becomes magnificent. It was placed at the top of a bank, with a north wall behind it, as she felt the colours of the undersides of the leaves and the towering flower-spike were then more spectacular; it flowered more freely than any other she grew at the bottom of the ditch garden.

Symphytums were considered good for this style of garden, and she used them to carry an area of planting over a difficult period. Their evergreen habit allowed the large hairy stems to make impressive clumps. *Symphytum peregrinum* with pink buds and light blue flowers was a good plant which increased slowly. Like all the comfreys it had the reputation of helping weakly plants to grow, particularly if they belonged to the potato family. *S. caucasicum* spread and seeded, its small grey-green leaves set off by flowers of gentian blue. Having found a magnificent variegated form, she realised that this was a perfect foil and companion for the variegated comfrey *Symphytum officinale* and the crimson-flowered taller form of great vigour.

To grow the prophet flower *Arnebia echioides* in shade on heavy clay is the achievement of a great gardener. The dark purple spots on the yellow flowers were reputed to disappear before rain! As a yellow borage it was not an unusual plant, but it needs poor dry soil and a harsh sunny situation to achieve the easy perennial habit so many gardeners claim for it and never quite achieve.

Margery liked the effect of silver plumes waving over fernlike foliage, though she considered *Boccania cordata* too invasive to plant with *Aruncus sylvester*, the old *Spiraea aruncus* or goat's beard. Aruncus looked well if viewed from a distance in front of the silver plumes of cortaderia, the Victorian pampas grass. She noticed pampas grass with approval on many garden visits: at Sheffield Park in the autumn, against brilliant red leaves where the colours reflected in the water, at Abbotswood in Gloucestershire in broad landscape and at Abbotsbury in Dorset as a hedge under trees. She grew the dwarf pampas grass *Cortaderia argentea (selloana)* Pumila at the top of a flight of steps in the ditch garden, beneath an apple tree, giving interest from September to December. The normal pampas grass needed a wider landscape; she tried many and found Sunningdale Silver the best for height. Where a change of colour was called for the soft pink plumes of *Cortaderia argentea* Rendatleri were a pleasant variation. Every April each clump was set on fire to tidy up the dead leaves, so the plumes displayed themselves against clean foliage. Cardoon or *Cynara cardunculus*, that little-known relative of the globe artichoke, with bold silver-green leaves, and in autumn royal purple flowers, is another magnificent plant and its personality is strong enough to impose on its neighbours. With seed heads of silver thistledown 7ft high, no clump could be ignored.

Some varieties of cimicifuga or bugbane have a peculiar smell, and have the reputation of carrying an insecticide; nonetheless they are good garden plants for shady, moist conditions. The strongest smelling, *Cimicifuga foetida intermedia*, has greenish-yellow flowers over pale green leaves, 3ft high, the best form being White Pearl. *Cimicifuga americana* is taller with leaves like a maple and tapering spikes of cream flowers on naked stems. The foliage of *Cimicifuga dahurica* is small and ferny, setting off the fluffy panicles of flowers tinged with blue, and the tallest, *C. ramosa*, grew 6ft high with 12–18in white flower spikes on slender stems.

'THE PERFECT WOODLAND GARDEN'

Margery loved the woodland gardens at Knightshayes, Devon, and at
A.T. Johnson's in North Wales (see Appendix). She never planted even
a copse at East Lambrook, and realised that people have different ideas
on what a woodland garden should be. Her own idea of perfection was
a garden made in a woodland setting with most of the undergrowth
cleared. Then the best of the woodland plants would be retained to
be shown off without coarser neighbours to detract from their charm.
Margery agreed with Mrs C.W. Earle that plants left to themselves
met certain death.

The nearest she ever attained in describing the ideal woodland
garden was when she placed her personal plantings against an imag-
ined background like the Savill Gardens in Windsor Great Park. She
liked this garden because it grew a wide range of plants for acid soils
that she could never grow at home. It had the added enchantment of
a stream winding under trees to give glimpses stretching away into the
distance. All of this she and Walter had hoped to achieve when they first
constructed the ditch garden at East Lambrook, which failed for lack of
water. She liked to see small bridges and shallow waterfalls, with iris,
primulas, lysichitum and other bog plants growing on the edge of the
water almost naturally.

She believed that the maintenance of a woodland garden needed
real artistry to keep it looking natural without being too untidy, or the
good plants losing their shape and being overgrown by more rampant
neighbours. The earth needed weeding, and suckers checking almost
invisibly, or the important ground cover would encroach to make the
whole a jungle. Grass growing naturally was acceptable in controlled
areas, but the long wait for the leaves of the spring bulbs to die down
was too high a price to pay for a controlled woodland garden. She liked
the idea of small beds for choice plants along the paths, because totally
wild planting meant that only plants like symphytums, foxgloves and
sweet rocket which were big enough to be cut round were safe from
the rough and tumble.

The plants which could be left to grow happily in grass that
is scythed once or twice a season were those that die down after

flowering. The martagon lilies growing in the woodland garden at St John's College, Cambridge, were an example. She felt she would add in *Lilium pyrenaicum* for a touch of gold, camassias for their pale blue haze, and *Gladiolus byzantinus* for a toning contrast. In fairly damp shade the native *Fritillaria meleagris* grows satisfactorily. A planting she admired in a friend's garden was of the white fritillary mixed with white narcissi, and the pale green *Fritillaria pyrenaica* as a contrast. This plant is a good naturaliser for wild gardens, tolerating more sun and drought than other fritillaries.

Under trees and at the edge of paths she liked to see plantings of snowdrops and aconites for the spring; an edge of gold and silver is never wrong, she frequently remarked. Later these plantings could merge into *Erythronium dens-canis*, muscari and anemones *blanda* and *apennina*. Silver birch and the tall Spanish bluebell, *Endymion hispanicus*, were superb planted together.

These were natural denizens of a woodland garden. Rarer treasures would distract attention from the range of colours on leaves created by the contrast of sun and shade.

THE SEMI-WILD GARDEN

During her lecturing and travelling Margery had seen many gardens which had native orchids coming in from the wild to grow in open woodland conditions. This was the type of plant she would have liked to grow in those small cultivated beds in the woodland garden of her dreams. *Orchis maculata* could be grown satisfactorily, but no other. She would have added such plants as her hose-in-hose cowslip or her crimson cowslip mixed with some of the less vigorous colchicums. Cowslips are more capricious than primroses, and she advocated growing only the wild primrose in grass.

A wide range of plants could be included in these semi-wild gardens within woodland: the double-flowering cardamine or lady's smock, double primroses and buttercups, jack-in-the-green and gold-laced poly-anthus. Brunnera, trachystemon and large clumps rather than colonies of hellebores would add to the charm of the trilliums which could not grow well at East Lambrook. Some of the species of herbaceous and tree paeony could be included to advantage. *P. officinalis* in crimson, pink

and white, with *peregrina* and *mascula* would look well combined with the tree paeonies *lutea ludlowii* and *delavayi*, the woodland hiding their ungainly branches when their leaves fell. The paeonies would tolerate lime but the blue Tibetan poppy *Meconopsis betonicifolia* needed an acid soil. More lime-tolerant but less striking were *Meconopsis regia* with hairy gold foliage, *simplicifolia* with single violet flowers, and *cambrica*, the golden Welsh poppy.

In all the woodland gardens she saw there was usually little difficulty in planting under most trees, provided the soil was well dug and supplied with humus. Many trees had an affinity with the correct ground cover. The evergreen Mediterranean oak *Quercus ilex* would drop a few leaves in late summer, and *Cyclamen neapolitanum* rapidly flower amongst them. Beech trees with their bad reputation provided perfect cover for the white helleborine *Cephalanthera damasonium*; other plants she saw succeeding under beeches were cyclamen with the dwarf anemones *blanda* and *apennina*, *Arum italicum* Pictum, and the Gladwyn iris, *Iris foetidissima*.

Elm trees seemed the most difficult for ground cover, and Margery thought well-planted ivies were the most satisfactory here – a wide range of variegation is obtainable in the numbers of Victorian culti-vars. Conifers were relatively easy to please – in the garden *Euphorbia cyparissias*, violets and variegated periwinkles grew beneath the now famous 'pudding trees'. For alternative plantings she grew *Geranium macrorrhizum*, with *Stachys lanata*, *Lathyrus latifolius*, *Lithospermum purpureo-caeruleum*, and the cream-flowered *Symphytum grandiflorum*.

A woodland garden should not be used as a repository for plants and shrubs which did not quite fit in the garden. Trees like the wild spin-dle *Euonymus europaeus*, the variegated elders and silver birches, were valuable there, and a woodland garden could take some good plants too robust for elsewhere, like the coarser doronicums and polemoniums; with pulmonarias, ajugas and the stronger-growing geraniums, they could be incorporated into lower ground cover without spoiling the overall effect of the natural woodland setting. Outside the small culti-vated beds would be plants such as tradescantia, the spiderwort, which would grow in the shade and give a long flowering period in pink, red, purple and white, with every shade of blue. The line of the planting could be broken with the lettuce *Lactuca bourgaei*, with the giant pars-ley or cartwheel plant *Heracleum mantegazzianum* and the single sweet

rocket in lilac and white. Honeysuckles and clematis would festoon the small bridges of the stream, and climb gently to the tree tops and the sunshine. Deep shade by the stream would accommodate some of the more attractive ferns like hart's tongue and the shield fern, while in the lighter shade primulas, meadowsweet and lythrum (loosestrife) would grow towards the foxgloves. Elder would mix with a flowering cherry, and wild mint provide a backdrop for the most exotic of Asiatic primulas.

BULBS AND CORMS IN THE WILDER GARDEN

As already seen, the soil at East Lambrook was not suitable for a wide range of bulbs, and as Margery always demanded that her plants must grow well, Asiatic lilies, for instance, were almost barred to her. Nonetheless she persisted with such bulbs as nerines and sternbergia for the benefit of their autumn flowers, and realised a shady, informal part of the garden was ideal for growing a wide range of bulbs and corms.

Unwittingly she grasped that the narcissus-fly does not like shade, and this made the propagation of some of the rarer daffodils easier. She was dealing with cultivars of which not more than 100 bulbs probably existed. She could not realise that the daffodils she was collecting from cottage gardens as she lectured would become so highly regarded within twenty years of her death.

In her ditch garden for the spring, in light shade, she planted *Narcissus bulbocodium* and early hybrids of *Narcissus cyclamineus* such as February Gold and Peeping Tom. She gave Queen Anne's double daffodil *Narcissus capax* Plenus its ideal conditions, and found the double jonquil, the Queen of Spain, *Narcissus nanus, canaliculatus* and N. × Minicycla with the cream W.P. Milner and white Thalia did equally well, and increased in quantity beyond her expectations.

Dry soil under shallow roots of trees provides a home for very few plants except ivies. Hardy cyclamen were better in slightly raised beds of humus-rich soil, and it became quite common to plant a wider range of bulbs and tubers like this; in one garden she saw that a bed had been created with old railway sleepers to house a collection of erythroniums. The commonest of these, *Erythronium dens-canis*, the dog's tooth violet, a wild flower of European woods with green and purple mottled leaves,

has a short flowering period, but has an attractive colour range from white to pink and lavender. It was easy to grow and seeded itself under the trees in grass at East Lambrook. The better colours, such as Snow-flake, Pink Perfection, Rose Beauty and the violet Frans Hals, grew in the ditch garden with the taller more exotic species from America. *Erythronium revolutum* (trout lily) in rose-pink and white, and *tuolumnense* in golden-yellow and able to tolerate drier conditions, two species she particularly enjoyed, reached almost 18in tall; their upturned petals in April and early May reminded her of a martagon lily. *E. californicum* in creamy-white and *grandiflorum* in golden-yellow were two further species grown, but never with the enthusiasm reserved for snowdrops, which with their early appearance and wide variation gave her special joy in the spring.

Snowdrops usually grow well in shade, but some of the rarer named varieties have vagaries which need learning by trial and error. All the autumn-flowering snowdrops, such as *reginae-olgae, cilicius* and *corcyrensis*, need a warm position and a good baking when dormant to flower satisfactorily; she never attempted to grow them other than in the sun. For naturalising under trees she preferred the ordinary single and double snowdrops. Named varieties were grown separately where they could be seen as clumps, or in raised beds, such as her three-sided troughs against the east wall of the Malthouse, where they showed the beauty of their leaves and arching stems.

Several small anemones grew in the shade, and some increased from being good ground cover to almost weeds. Anemones *blanda, apennina* and *nemorosa* in shades of white and blue were easy to plant in shady borders for March colour, but some of the named forms of *nemorosa* were too precious to be given this treatment: the large lavender-blue flowers of Allenii and Robinsoniana, the single white Vestal with its centre of petaloid anthers, and the double white. The easy *Anemone ranunculoides superba* Flore Pleno was an acquisition treasured for some years.

Anemone sylvestris needed care. A deep rich soil in shade suited it best, and with its 15in stems, and pleasant scent in spring, it was worth the trouble. A good companion plant was the soft blue *Scilla messeniaca*, 6in high in soft pale blue, its only problem being that it grew too strongly and had to be stopped before the stems died to a lank unpleasant yellow. Margery's favourite scilla was *tubergeniana*. Flowering in February in Wedgwood blue with a turquoise stripe, it

was planted in every dull corner possible.

Grape hyacinths became a weed at East Lambrook, but Margery weakened and left some to seed in the middle of her most cared-for treasures. The choicer or less ordinary types were much easier to control. The small white form of *Hyacinthus azureus* never seeded, nor indeed did the Cambridge-blue type. *Muscari paradoxum* was almost black and *latifolium* grew with flowers of pale blue over dark blue. These, with the small *racemosum* in deep navy blue, *neglectum* in blue-black, *viridis* in greenish-blue, and *moschatum flavum* which started in purple and ended pale yellow, grew happily in shade. They were complemented by the feathery grape hyacinth *Muscari comosum monstrosum*, and the green of the purple-topped type *comosum*.

Colchicums grow well under trees, and they were planted in grass in the orchard. There are a large number of species and named hybrids and they were mixed by height, colour and season. To do this she used *Colchicum autumnale album* and *autumnale* Flore Pleno, *Colchicum speciosum rubrum* and *album*, with the dwarf chequered lilac-purple *agrippinum*. The named hybrids dating from Edwardian gardens like Violet Queen, Autumn Queen, The Giant, Lilac Wonder and light blue Disraeli were mixed with the double-flowering Water Lily, providing brilliant colour on a mild autumn day.

The true crocus, particularly the autumn and winter flowering, are not really happy in shade, but *byzantinus* and *speciosus* were planted in light shade. For naturalising, she preferred groups of single colours; purple went with white, and white with yellow, but yellow and purple were better not mixed.

Hardy cyclamen were best in shade, dry or damp, even sowing themselves into the roots of trees. *Cyclamen neapolitanum*, *neapolitanum album* and *repandum* grew at the base of the *Lonicera nitida* hedges, and the white were separated from the pink when in full flower. The long-term aim, never achieved, was a band of cyclamen under every hedge for the autumn. Top-dressed with peat before flowering, they increased and seeded, but never quickly enough for East Lambrook's needs. *Repandum* grew as happily in shade as *neapolitanum*; she would also grow her winter-flowering cyclamen in shade under small cypresses. The more tender *Cyclamen graecum*, *africanum*, *europaeum* and *pseudibericum* grew better in a warm sunny place on a rockery.

Even on the terraces looking towards the barton, carefully controlled self seeding created the effect of a natural garden

The star of Bethlehem, *Ornithogalum umbellatum*, gives the ornithogalum family a bad name, but in Margery's eyes they had one great virtue – flowers of green and white, a colour combination she particularly liked. Some of the species would grow satisfactorily in the garden, and usefully helped fill the May gap. Her primary choice was *Ornithogalum nutans* with its flower of silvery-grey combined with a pale green. She considered the two tall ones, *Ornithogalum arabicum* and *pyramidale*, with their spikes of snowy blossom to be as good in a shady border as the larger white snowdrop blossoms of *Galtonia candicans*; this plant's near relative, *Galtonia princeps*, was a favourite flower in the green garden in light shade, accompanied by the pale green stems of *Zigadenus elegans*.

The green garden was greatly helped by fritillaries, principally the greenish-gold of *Fritillaria pyrenaica* (the only one that would naturalise in grass in the orchard as the native *meleagris* does). In the shade of other plants she also grew *pontica*, green with a brown edge; it needed to be

seen at eye-level, for Margery liked the black nectaries inside glowing green petals. *Ruthenica* had greenish mottling on browny-black; the pale yellow *bithynica* and *pudica* did not live long at East Lambrook; *pallidiflora* had large creamy bells, and *acmopetala* was greenish-yellow and maroon. *Fritillaria persica*, 3ft tall with grape-coloured flowers, shared with *Fritillaria imperialis* pride of place in Parkinson's great Stuart gardening book; she planted it for late spring height at various points in the garden. Like *Fritillaria imperialis* the bulb needs tilting to avoid moisture rotting the centre. Margery always regretted never growing the variegated crown imperial as E.A. Bowles did under trees at Myddleton House, Enfield, when she first visited his garden. She grew crown imperials in yellow, orange, copper and rusty-red, but never the one she coveted most.

Just after the war several forms of *Fritillaria meleagris* were selected, and named – incongruously since it is a native of Northern Europe – after Greek gods. These became the best fritillaries for light shade, and were planted in beds with lily-of-the-valley and *martagon*, *regale* and *pyrenaicum* lilies; she never trusted these rare and special forms to the orchard for naturalising, as she did the unnamed seedlings in mixed shades from white to chequered purple. Among the named forms were the large white Aphrodite, Poseidon in chequered white veined purple, Artemis in soft grey and purple, Suphanus in cream and mauve, and Saturnus which was chequered as near pink as a fritillary could be. Margery thought that by the 1980s we should have some 50 named varieties: the flower colours varied so much in the fritillary meadows she visited. She recalled that before the First World War the Dutch grew this number. But even the few named varieties of her day have slowly slipped from nurserymen's lists.

In the heavy clay, *regale* lily was pleased most easily; some other lilies, including Bellingham hybrids, were happy with the lime in the soil; *auratum*, *speciosum* and *longiflorum* were not, while *candidum* grew well in an open position in sun. This planting was dull after mid-summer, so schizostylis were added, in three forms of red – *coccinea*, Professor Barnard and *coccinea major*, with two forms of pink Mrs Hegarty and the paler Viscountess Byng. They flowered from October to December, so constant pleasure was given throughout the year from one planting in one space, the very essence of her gardening objectives.

11

The Garden in Spring

Valerie Finnis, a successful photographer and member of staff at Waterperry Horticultural School, later became a more famous gardener as Lady Scott of Boughton House, Kettering. Her photographs of Margery, her plants and garden, remain as tangible evidence of their longstanding friendship. The first time she arrived at East Lambrook village she asked the way to Mrs Fish's garden, wondering how Margery could live in a village with such a noise of jazz music: then she saw Margery emerge and the noise stopped. Margery explained she had been writing and liked to have a background to her thoughts.

Margery might not have so successfully extended the use of flowers throughout the year without the help of Valerie Finnis, whose encyclopedic knowledge of the actual flowering time of so many plants complemented her own ideas. Their mutual interest in hellebores naturally enough started the gardening year in January. Their plantings of the various species led to more being grown, as already seen.

Margery's considered view was that a good garden was a winter garden, because the other three seasons brought their own rewards. Stems, seed heads, form and flowers were all used to create winter interest. 'The flowers we do have are very precious; in fact one flower in winter is worth a hundred at any other time of the year, but there are other ways of making the garden attractive in winter' *(A Flower for Every Day)*. At this season there was time to 'look into the flowers and study them'.

IRIS AND CYCLAMEN

The small flowers of January were herbaceous, usually bulbs and tubers like iris species, at that time relatively uncommon. *Iris unguicularis (stylosa)*, in blue or white, is easy if given a good baking in the summer; but the dwarf forms of *Iris histrio* and *histrioides* were

never found reliably perennial; *alata* and *vartanii* usually flowered once and abandoned the unequal struggle with heavy clay, wind and wintry rain. She particularly enjoyed *Iris danfordiae* with its beaming flowers of dandelion yellow, and eventually took to potting it up to ensure her complement of flowers. On asking a Dutch grower how they produced bulbs to flower each year, she was told it was no problem in their rich soil. The secret with this bulb is growing it about 18in above water in good soil, and then baking it. Eventually a backing of the bronzed ferny leaves of *Corydalis cheilanthifolia* was used to thicken the planting. *Iris reticulata* bloomed in February: the ordinary form had a better scent than the newer coloured forms such as Cantab or the rich red-purple J.S. Dijt, and was the only one to be reliably perennial for Margery.

The dwarf *Iris histrioides* was an excellent companion for the aconites *Eranthis hyemalis* growing under a variegated sycamore on the lawn. After a while she experimented with the less common aconites, like *cilicica* with deep yellow flowers and a touch of bronze in its Elizabethan ruff of leaves. *Eranthis tubergenii* is a hybrid of the first two, with larger, showier, long-lasting flowers and a sturdier habit of growth; the form Guinea Gold has deep gold flowers on bronze stems and is scented. Margery never attempted the white Japanese aconite, *E. pinnatifida*, with its blue anthers and blue-backed petals: it needed shade, a light, acid, well-drained soil and no slugs.

The hardy winter cyclamen pleased Margery because flowers and leaves come together. Their nomenclature was suspect even before they were all called *Cyclamen coum* hybrids. She had *C. hiemale, vernum, atkinsii* and *coum*, with *ibericum*, only to find their seedlings totally indistinguishable; when showing visitors round the garden in January she referred to them as her unlawful children. They grew under her 'pudding trees' along the central path, as she felt they liked the shade and were less likely to be disturbed. *Cyclamen neapolitanum* grew under the shade of a hedge of *Lonicera nitida* in the upper part of the garden so the marbling of the leaves could be seen from the path in winter; and their neat clusters of flowers and leaves in all shades in the heart of winter on the lower terrace never failed to please. From white to pink or magenta, the flowers grew on erect stems above the leaves in all the varieties that did not claim to be *coum*. Here the buds on long stems lay on the ground, taking a long time to open, giving a rather straggling effect; the plant was untidy in its magenta form though it looked pleasant in grass. The

The ditch garden in spring was a memorable sight

white and pink were better, and in one of the trough gardens a white one flowered from Christmas until Easter, nestling happily among the stones. The winter-flowering varieties did not colonise an area as well as the autumn and spring varieties, although Margery knew gardens where under mulberry, ilex and beech with lack of competition they seeded more happily. The problem one was *pseudibericum*, which seemed reluctant to flower, despite its hardiness in cold winters. On a visit to a garden at Porlock, she noticed a well-grown flowering specimen with its corm planted under a stone; she found three more corms, planted them under stones on high banks facing south in the ditch garden, and they flowered with complete success.

PERIWINKLES AND HELLEBORES

As January progressed the clear blue flowers appearing on the periwinkles *Vinca minor* and *major* made her forgive them for their later invasiveness. One for reliable winter flowers was *Vinca difformis* or *acutiloba*, the Mediterranean periwinkle, which needs a good warm

position and kind weather to make its pale slaty-blue flowers work up a bank or wall. In an open bed it will grow about 1ft high and proceed to flower; under a tree it does better, since it fancies itself as a climber – though a bad frost will blacken its leaves. In Italy it is used for bedding, and in England in Edwardian times it gained a reputation as a cool-house pot plant. The brilliant blue La Graveana and Bowles' White *Vinca minor* were usually flowering by March. Nowadays the Bowles' White is often referred to as Miss Jekyll's form, as she was the original possessor of the plant. The double-flowered *minor* Rubra Flore Pleno and double blue were also appearing in March.

More hellebores bloomed with each day of January. *H. kochii* and *atrorubens* would begin, along with *lividus*, *corsicus* and *foetidus* in their separate forms. Some varieties of *orientalis* would begin to come to life but this, with *niger*, was really a flower of February. So were *Helleborus sternii*, a cross between *corsicus* and *lividus*, and *cyclophyllus* with its large perfectly formed green flowers, deeper in colour than *corsicus*, but lighter than *viridis*. These hellebores were presented better as single clumps rather than drifts. With the species hellebores were mixed such hybrids as Prince Rupert, with heavy maroon stippling in its pale moonlight-green cups. The darkest of all is Apotheker Bogren, with Black Knight and Ballard's Black. Doubts about the parents of *H. torquatus* – not a species but a hybrid – showed in the variations of its flowers; all were shades of bluish-purple, small and lightly waved, but only *torquatus* has so far provided a double form for commerce. These variations that fascinated Margery crept into *H. abschasicus*, in lighter shades of reddish-purple. The more exposed positions were given to the Lenten roses or *Helleborus orientalis*, in all their colours, from white to purple. Margery liked these hellebores planted under winter-flowering shrubs, such as the witch hazels – *Hamamelis mollis* in medium yellow, the paler *H.m.* Pallida, Brevipetala with its deep ochre-yellow or rich *H. x itermedia* Ruby Glow, and Adonis in burnt umber. Hiltingbury Red was a form of Japanese witch hazel, *Hamamelis japonica*, with flowers of rich mahogany-red. The restful grey-green of *Garrya elliptica*, with its long strings of flowers of cream and green, was a useful contrast to the witch hazels' yellows and oranges. Margery preferred Garrya grown against a wall, because a sharp frost blackened the leaves; probably it needed better drainage than her heavy clay provided, and with dry roots it would be able to stand more frost. It has little scent, but it did add

height to the garden in winter. Sarcococcas remained neat little ever-green bushes, with tiny cream flowers scented with honey and vanilla; as obliging members of the euphorbia family they grew happily under trees and shrubs, away from *Chimonanthus fragrans* whose scent did not mix well with theirs. Chimonanthus, both *fragrans* and *grandiflorus*, were January favourites; seeing the yellow flowers of *C. luteus* shining against a wall in sunshine after rain at the Savill Gardens remained a grey-day pleasure. *Daphne blagayana's* scented cream flowers were also reliable January arrivals.

FAIR MAIDS OF FEBRUARY

If the sun shone on Candlemas day, 2 February, Margery would repeat 'If it be fine on Candlemas day, the worst of winters to come your way,' and went off to see the snowdrops or Candlemas bells. *Galanthus elwesii* and the small *graecus* with its twisted leaves were usually the first to flower, and were soon followed by the common snowdrop, *G.nivalis*, under the apple trees; then by the dwarf double Pusey Green Tip, and the taller single *nivalis* Viridapicis. By the middle of February many forms of *Galanthus plicatus* were flowering; her favourite was Warham.

The single yellow snowdrop, *G. nivalis lutescens*, found by a Cam-bridge seedsman, Mr Saunders, in an old Northumberland garden, never grew well, and consequently she fussed it too much; it needs full sun and good drainage, and to put it in a trough did not help either. Nor should it be allowed to seed, as the seedlings come green and crowd out the parent. The double yellow snowdrop Lady Elphinstone, named by Sam Arnott after the owner of Harwood Hall, Cheshire, where it was found, was a better grower, and increased successfully if given shade, moisture and humus.

Fellow enthusiasts Brigadier and Mrs Matthias of Chalford, Glou-cestershire, identified one of her best early doubles with a totally green centre as H.A. Greatorex's hybrid Ophelia. This flower lifts its outer petals so they resemble cyclamen for a short period. They developed a passionate interest in snowdrops after they bought the garden of the late Walter Butt, which contained many rare cultivars that had multiplied after his death. They bred new varieties, formed the Giant Snowdrop Company, and sought out and redistributed many old forms.

Their enthusiasm and their joy in Margery's articles on snowdrops in *Amateur Gardening* and *The Field* created a long friendship between them. After their deaths, Ranson, who had been their chauffeur, took over the distribution, and the famous large scented February snowdrop Sam Arnott, bred by Walter Butt, became available to every interested gardener. By the time Margery concluded gardening she was growing some 60 varieties of snowdrops, with at least 25 in her nursery list; but nurseries which specialise in snowdrops today offer at least 100.

The Straffan snowdrop is named from Straffan House on the River Liffey, where the Hon Mrs Barton received some bulbs from her brother Lord Clarina who was serving in the Crimea. One bulb produced two flowers and was such a good plant it was selected; from it all the Straffan snowdrops were grown. Over the years slight variations occurred, all of which Margery grew. E.A. Bowles had one at Myddleton House; the McMarney Straffan was another, with two more that had small touches of green and slightly longer stems.

Also among them was the 10in John Grey, its flowers rather clumsier than those of the slightly smaller and earlier Sam Arnott. Mr Bowles told her that many of the snowdrops grown in Britain were sent back from the trenches of the Crimean War, but the double green-centred form of *Galanthus plicatus* was similar to Ophelia, one of the Greatorex doubles. *Galanthus elwesii, caucasicus* and *elwesii whittallii* have similar wide grey-green leaves, with flowers slightly different in shape and green markings.

Fortunately, galanthomania, as Tony Venison of *Country Life* terms the collection of innumerable named varieties that hardly differ, did not grip Margery. She preferred the species, and grew the donkey-eared *G. nivalis* Scharlockii, and *allenii* with broad yellow-green leaves, while *ikariae ikariae* and *ikariae latifolius* finished the flowering season in late March. What she did collect were some very distinct varieties of the wild snowdrop. *Galanthus nivalis* Magnet, its flowers swaying on a long curved pedicil, and two stems from a bulb, was one; she frequently wrote about it in garden magazines, and sold it in her nursery. Double snowdrops held their petals longer and many of them were planted: Hill Poe and Miss Hassell's Double were two she popularised, along with the green-centred single Merlin, Colesborne with green-edged white, Virescens with green in and out, and the Bowles' miniature he called Norfolk.

The snowdrops were planted in little colonies on the shady side of the

ditch, with larger leaves to provide a colour contrast. Crimson *Bergenia delavayi* and *purpurascens*, and the bright shiny foliage of *Fatshedera lizei* contrasted with the glistening flowers of *Galanthus elwesii*. All the pulmonarias in pink and blue were used, but the silver-leaved *Pulmonaria argentea* was saved for the green-leaved *Galanthus ikariae.*

The closely allied snowflakes, *Leucojum vernum* in green and *carpathicum* in yellow, were mixed with the marbled leaves of *Arum italicum* Pictum and the fluttering leaves of epimedium, and with *Iris unguicularis* in such forms as the pale, scented Walter Butt, the white Alba, Mary Barnard in deep violet, and the bluest of all, Ellisii. All the snowflakes grow well in shade; *Leucojum vernum*, which with its green points looks like a grander snowdrop, and *carpathicum* both flowered in early spring with the aconites and snowdrops. The summer snowflake *Leucojum aestivum* is probably the best for the garden, growing some 18 to 24in tall, particularly *L.aestivum* Gravetye Giant. Its flowers hanging on long pedicils always looked well when picked and arranged against the panelling at East Lambrook. Margery grew the little 3in autumn snowflake in troughs or the rock garden; it increased quickly, but she found it was less tolerant of lime than the two earlier-flowering leucojums, and rather less hardy as well.

There would have been more colour in the winters, she admitted, if she had enjoyed winter heathers. She used the mauve-pink flowers of *Erica carnea* under the blue-grey conifer in the rock garden, lightened by the silvery ferny leaves of *Centaurea gymnocarpa*. Another form of *carnea* with gold leaves and white flowers crouched under a stone near the gold and green mottled leaves of *Bellis aucubaefolia*; nearby the mottled leaves of *Lonicera japonica* Aureoreticulata were tinted crimson as they tumbled among the crimson leaves of a self-sown antirrhinum. The best form of heather was the acid-loving *Calluna vulgaris* Mrs Pat. In silver-bright pink it filled the front of a greensand bed dominated by the dark shining leaves of *Pyrola rotundifolia* and *Rhododendron repens*.

EYE-LEVEL COLOUR FROM SHRUBS

During February height would be added by *Cornus mas*, in its variegated form, with its tiny yellow flowers; and *Mahonia japonica*, its spikes of scented flowers getting shorter as the leaves began to turn crimson.

Pink was contributed in any mild spell from September to April by *Prunus subhirtella* Autumnalis. A planting Margery admired was where this grew on a bank, underplanted with *Lamium galeobdolon* Variegatum in grey and silver; at East Lambrook it was underplanted with spring snowflake, and was successful for a month, but the lamium was there for twelve. Continued green came from *Ribes laurifolium*, with its pale green flowers and dark glossy leaves, planted against a north wall with hostas, hellebores and the blue and fernlike *Acaena adscendens*, a robust plant that swirled over the paths and softened hard corners of stonework.

Daphne laureola, spurge laurel, had unobtrusive green flowers but they offered scent at the end of the day. March was usually the month of *Daphne odora*, but the white and crimson-purple forms of *Daphne mezereum* were usually well in evidence by the middle of February. The long rigid primrose pearls of *Stachyurus praecox* and *chinensis* hung from bare boughs with reddish bark, complementing the small *Forsythia ovata*, and the tallest forsythia, *giraldiana*.

On the east wall *Prunus mume* Beni-shidon flowered in deep pink, sweetly scented and heavily stamened; added interest was given by a large patch of golden-variegated ivy. Margery continued to use bare stems, seed heads and grasses, many of which by this time had bleached into pale ivory; not every visitor enjoyed this effect, many commenting later that the effect was like a jungle. For example every branch of the 'wiggly willow' *Salix matsudana* Tortusa, and every twisted stem of the corkscrew hazel *Corylus contorta*, were carefully placed as focal points before their leaves covered their eccentricity.

One of the garden rules was to cut *Clematis jackmanii* on 15 February, buds and all; then new shoots would grow quickly, with less risk of clematis wilt. If the thick old stems broke off, they would usually grow from the bottom at ground level. Ville de Lyon and the *viticella* group accepted the same treatment; from Blue Gem, Henryi and others of the *lanuginosa* group only the dead wood was removed. Drastic treatment seemed to suit *Clematis tangutica* and *rehderiana* as they raced up the wall the following spring. Margery was careful never to touch *macropetala* and only restrained the *montanas* by wire netting nailed to the wall.

On the lawn, *Acer pseudoplatanus leopoldii* burst into colour with the spring

SEED HEADS, LEAVES AND STEMS

The large leaves of a form of *Bergenia cordifolia* turned crimson in winter and were used against the bright brown seed heads of *Sedum telephium*, with silver *Stachys lanata* behind; the orange and gold of the leaves of *Bergenia crassifolia* were planted with *Santolina incana*. *Bergenia schmidtii* with dark leaves was the first to flower. The rich crimson leaves of *B. delavayi* and *B. purpurascens* were complemented by the green-and-cream striped leaves of *Iris foetidissima* Variegata, or the tougher silver leaves of *Senecio laxifolius*. *Senecio monroi* is not so silver, its grey leaves, white below, showing to advantage against the rich red-brown stems of physostegia, Summer Spire, while the white leaves of *Olearia mollis* completed the picture. The white stems of *Perowskia atriplicifolia* waved behind the ruddy seed heads of *Sedum* Autumn Joy. Margery did not cut down stems of good colour or stems of herbaceous plants which looked like deciduous shrubs once their flowering was over.

The branching stems of *Althaea cannabina* reached 8 to 10ft tall, and *Eupatorium purpureum* grew 6 to 8ft in a thicket of dark stems when its flat purple flowers were complete. *Serratula coronata* with purple thistle-flowers on stout stems was always kept, as were the teasels, which Margery liked better when brown on a snowy day than when flowering in soft lavender. February was the month of promise. Pink tips of paeonies and fresh green veratrum mingled with the blue-grey of mertensia and the closely packed buds of mandrakes. Margery admitted she died a hundred deaths until she saw her old friends returning safely. It is worth remembering how few plants of difficult nature or doubtful hardiness were ever given prominence at East Lambrook.

MARCH BEGINS THE GROWING SEASON

In March the growing and flowering season began in earnest. Some of the large euphorbias opened, the tall *wulfenii* with orange eyes followed by *sibthorpii* with brown eyes, and the smallest and neatest, *characias*, with beady black eyes. Elsewhere *Helleborus corsicus* had the large, rare

Euphorbia androsacinifolia and *E. valdevilloscarpa* as a background, which enhanced the grey-green leaves and green flowers.

Brunnera macrophylla, with grey-green leaves and bright blue flowers, received sufficient cover from a white geum and *Epimedium sulphureum* to hide the winter's treatment of its leaves. The flowers of the omphalodes are bigger than the brunnera's, and the glossy foliage of *Omphalodes cappadocica* never gets out of hand. They liked a shady moist position between stones at the edge of a north wall, complementing cyclamen or lavender primroses as edging plants. The earliest omphalodes to flower is *verna*, blue-eyed Mary, which sometimes began at the end of February at East Lambrook, and by early March showed plenty of flowers, as did the white-flowered form, Margery's favourite when in a narrow border with anthericums or pink dentaria. *Omphalodes luciliae* flowers later and is more difficult; its blue leaves and porcelain-blue flowers were placed in shade, hanging down from the rockery crevices.

The first single primrose to flower was usually *Primula* Wanda, which she grew in the shade to mute the metallic purple sheen of the flower. The lavender colours were more easily placed. Mrs McGillivary, with mauve-pink flowers on polyanthus stems, is twice the size of the tiny Mauve Queen; Fair Maid has a blue haze, and purple Jill has flat dark crinkled leaves with stems that root like the pink Kinlough Beauty. The cream polyanthus Lady Greer has such small leaves it was hardly visible before the flowers came. Frost affected the deep purples of Julius Caesar and Tawny Port, and the deep crimson of Dinah, Betty and David Green. Their colours returned as the month progressed.

BULBS AND CORMS IN SPRING

The self-seeding habit of chionodoxas and scillas seemed to encourage them into the warmest, most sheltered parts of the garden. The first to flower was the dwarf, pale blue *Scilla tubergeniana*, followed by the wide white eyes of the chionodoxas – the vivid blue of the common squill was the most satisfactory, rather than the paler blue, larger chionascilla, a cross between the two species. The paler scillas flowered later. *Scilla messinaica* was promiscuously vigorous; Margery frequently visited a garden at Porlock where it had covered large areas with sheets of blue, and acted as a contrast to the winter cyclamen. The darker *Scilla bifolia*

flowered later still and was a good coloniser; *Scilla azureus* in the same shade of blue appealed for its bluebell habit. The white scilla, the albino form of the common squill, grew in only one clump at East Lambrook and did not seed itself. It was encouraged, as was the white Snowdrift crocus, because of the shortage of good white flowers in March.

Late March brought the ditch garden to one of its loveliest times. The summer snowflake *Leucojum aestivum* Gravetye Giant flowered between the variegated and double Solomon's seal, while double camassia, bronze-leaved *Crocosmia (Montbretia)* Solfatare and libertias completed the planting. The plants with flowers hanging on arching stalks got the highest places so their full beauty was displayed; the small snowflake flowers looked best against a leafy background.

In Somerset, March is the month daffodils are at their best. Margery would observe their habit in nature, and then emulate it. In the wild they need to be in a good clump for the outline of the flowers to show against the background of the leaves. Daffodils grown together need a green backing if they are not to look garish – as they do in rows in bare earth. The most ordinary of them grown in clumps with grass as a background were better by far in her eyes than the rarest bulbs grown in a flower-bed with nursery neatness. In Margery's opinion everyone should be grateful to people who clump up their daffodils by the roadside or in drives by their houses. Only one daffodil looked better on its own – the Queen of Spain. The double-flowering cottage types of daffodil like Rip Van Winkle, Van Sion and Queen Anne, were joined by the single Tenby daffodil and King Alfred. As soon as the white-flowered ones appeared she lost interest in the gold, for flowers like Beersheba and Mount Hood were soft-coloured enough to work well in a flower bed and also indoors when picked. When planted in shade under trees, Thalia with two flowers to a stem looked well with the pale sulphur colour of W.P. Milner. The little daffodils, such as *Narcissus cyclamineus* and *bulbocodium*, needed a safe place to hold their own and grow. Indeed the only success of the peat garden for heathers was the way the dwarf daffodils grew there.

Gaps in the paving were coloured in March by *Iris chamaeiris*, with buds as tall as the leaves. In blue, purple, primrose and gold they contrasted with the grey paving stones. The later, taller, white forms Bride and Green Spot with the dwarfer Green Eyes were usually grown at the side of the path.

Thoughts of green turning into gold also came in March, with plants like *Euphorbia epithymoides (polychroma)* and *myrsinites*. These were usually planted with clumps of colchicum leaves. Here *Dondia (Hacquetia) epipactis* fitted the style of the garden for March: dwarf shamrock-leaved with green-gold flowers and conspicuous stamens, it was used as an edging to be later outshadowed by taller plants. It was among her favourite spring flowers, and she appreciated it as Eleanour Sinclair Rohde did in the previous generation of gardeners.

It did not suffer from exposure to frost as much as some of the bergenias, such as *ciliata*, which needed careful placing to avoid being browned. The ordinary kingcup, *Caltha palustris*, in its single, double and cream flowering forms, did well in good moist ground. As March drew to its close, the garden at East Lambrook became full of yellow and orange mixing together, with *Forsythia intermedia* Spectabilis, *suspensa*, dwarf *viridissima* Bronxensis and *ovata* in the more exposed positions, and the cream *Osmanthus delavayi*. Originally planted in a rather exposed position this flowered better when moved to a west-facing wall. Margery made every effort not to over-yellow the garden at this season, planting varieties in strategic places that were cream rather than butter-coloured. Nonetheless, she concluded that as March moved into April, the month she considered as the entrance to summer, she needed more shrubs to bring in pink to soften the yellow.

12

The Garden in Summer

As the days of April lengthened so the hellebores had their final blooming, *lividus, corsicus* and their hybrids setting their seed heads for their final contribution to the garden. *Helleborus orientalis* lived up to its reputation for promiscuity, and produced many seedlings which Margery sold from the nursery, including a greenish-cream one still available today which she named Greenland, the last to flower. The euphorbias continued in early April, with *wulfenii, sibthorpii* and *characias* flowering in the terrace garden. *Biglandulosa, myrsinites, polychroma* and *cyparissias* were then placed to get the maximum benefit of their autumn foliage. In 1960 over 30 different euphorbias were growing in the garden; this family fully repaid the space she gave them, and the articles she wrote in the gardening press made them far better known.

AUBRETIA, ALYSSUM AND ARABIS

Aubretia and *Alyssum saxatile* gave the April garden an unwanted purple and gold effect, but these two plants self-seeded no matter how hard she tried to avoid the poorer aubretias. By 1960 many of the newer seedings were in a wider range of colours, single, semi-double and double, but were not being reliably perennial, a problem shared with the delicate-coloured *Alyssum* Citrinum, or the soft biscuit Dudley Neville. Margery felt that to banish totally either the 'gold dust' of *Alyssum saxatile* or the mauve of aubretia would spoil her springtime cottage-garden colour, needed for interesting groupings with foliage.

The white arabis was another plant to tolerate rather than encourage, in the crevices of walls or paving; she preferred the shorter-lived pink forms, or occasionally the double white, which except for its lack of scent she considered as good as a perennial stock. In the walls, the deep red-purple of the rounded flower heads on stiff stems of *Arabis blepharophylla* was an unusual colour for April.

ANEMONES AND PRIMROSES

An abundance of primroses bloomed in the garden, over 200 varieties as well as the numerous seedlings from which she selected the named Lambrook varieties. Her eye for a good primrose never closed. When filling her car with petrol one day she saw a good crimson seedling primrose, charmed the plant from the garage owner, took it home and distributed it through the nursery as Lopen Red. Barrowby Gem and Bartimeus were two of her best difficult polyanthus: the scented lemon Barrowby Gem was raised by Mrs McColl in the late 1920s. Mrs McColl told Eleanour Sinclair Rohde in 1929 that she noticed it as a soft yellow seedling in her garden some years previously. After division it gave about a dozen plants and she collected seed from them. Out of the 200 seedlings, only one produced the same soft yellow flowers, but in a deeper shade. This plant was the original Barrowby Gem still grown today. The origin of Bartimeus, the old eyeless black polyanthus, is lost; it was probably a Georgian sport from a strain of gold-laced polyanthus. Margery always hoped to find either hose-in-hose or double flowers on some of the primroses and polyanthus, and just once a plant of Jill sported a double flower: she removed the small purple prize with care and transplanted it – it bloomed single the following year!

The anemones rivalled the primroses at this time of year, in their soft pastel shades of pink, white and blue, and happily naturalised. The season started with *Anemone blanda* and *apennina* to which in segregated care were added the dark blue *blanda atrocoerulea*, *Anemone blanda* Fairy in white, Rosea in clear pink and *scythinica*, white with a clear blue interior. The wood anemones in their cultivated forms, such as *Anemone nemorosa* Albaplena, *nemorosa* Allenii in soft blue, and the large Robinsoniana in lavender, took their place in shade. *Anemone pulsatilla*, the pasque flower of legend, in lavender, white, red and pink, flowered more vigorously each year as the fertility of the soil built up and improved the drainage of the clay.

In blocks at the front of a border, or in bands at the edge of a path, her well-loved hen-and-chickens daisies, and daisies such as Dresden China and its white counterpart The Pearl, Rob Roy, Alice

and such others as she could collect, were grown – including the speckled Bon Accord.

APRIL–MAY BULBS AND CORMS

Later daffodils were still flowering in April, and one which accumulated in the garden was Inglescombe. Its double flowers in lemony primrose reminded her of a primrose-coloured gardenia; she preferred it to many of the newer cultivars then becoming popular. *Erythronium dens-canis*, dog's-tooth violet, did not naturalise in the grass in the orchard, although it seeded itself in the peat garden; when transplanted the leaves were effective but they became shy to flower. The bright yellow *Erythronium californicum*, *E. dens-canis* Rose Queen and *E.tuolumnense* in rich yellow, or paler Cream Beauty, did best in shade, along with santolinas with their gentle grey foliage. This worked until the santolinas grew too big, when either they or the erythroniums had to be moved. Usually it was the erythroniums, as one of the maxims of Margery's gardening was not to scrap plants which got too big, because it levelled the garden. For all the plants to be small, neat, ordered and well tended made a dull garden in her view.

Iris bucharica, with satiny white and yellow flowers and pale green leaves, was used with the pale cobalt-blue of *Iris graeberiana* in well drained positions; they did not take kindly to her heavy soil.

Amongst shrubs where their unsightly foliage could be hidden but still close enough to a path so their scent could be enjoyed, was the pheasant eye, *Narcissus poeticus recurvis*, which Margery remembered from her childhood. The gardenia narcissus *(plenus odoratus)* was always the last to flower; it is the double form of *Narcissus poeticus*. To avoid the disappointment of empty flower buds this needs good moist soil in full sun. Naturalisation is only sometimes successful. *Muscari comosum plumosum*, the shaggy-headed 'plume hyacinth' with its fine feathery flowers of violet filaments was an easier bulb. Flowering in May in company with the green and white star of Bethlehem, *Ornithogalum umbellatum*, it helped create the right atmosphere for her style of gardening.

Colourful Shrubs and Trees

April can be a difficult month as the first flush of bloom fades, and the garden became planted with April-flowering shrubs and trees of predominantly pink colours to carry it into early summer. The ground gradually covered with the brightness of aubretia, arabis and alyssum, toned with the soft pastel shades of anemones and primroses.

Shrubs and trees dominated at this time. *Prunus subhirtella* Autumnalis was still flowering in early April, and when the season was kind *Viburnum utile* would continue its flat pale pink flower heads. This, one of the parents of *Viburnum burkwoodii*, (the other being *carlesii*) was not a widely grown shrub. Margery would have preferred it planted against a white background rather than the grey of the Malthouse east wall, but even this never detracted from its glory in flower. Equally the siting of the pink-flowered, purple-leaved sloe, *Prunus spinosa (cerasifera)* Rosea never satisfied her. She preferred it to be alone, so when turning a corner one could suddenly see it covered in pink blossom. Another shrub that did not have an ideal position was *Cytisus kewensis*, best seen pouring down over a wall like rich spilt cream. Only a light clipping of the ends was needed after flowering to keep it trim. It was past its best in May, but the upright *C.* Cornish Cream still flowered, with the taller White Pearl.

The flowering shrubs of May were mostly on a higher level in the garden than the early shrubs; they included lilac, deutzia and the pearl tree, *Exochorda racemosa*, dripping its strings of white flowers. This does not like a shallow chalk soil, and Margery advised gardeners with this to use *Exochorda serratifolia*, which would grow up to 12ft high. *Weigela middendorffiana*, with its sulphur-yellow flowers and dark orange linings on the lower lobes, needed sheltered shade to do well; *Weigela florida* in its variegated form was sufficiently compact to place among the herbaceous plants.

The golden racemes of laburnum streamed against the stone of the Malthouse in the distance: all laburnums, Margery felt, needed to be planted where their silhouette could be enjoyed, including the more exotic *autumnale* with occasional flowers until early autumn, or the oak-leaved *L. anagyroides* Quercifolium.

Cynara cardunculus dominated the long border in summer

Below a Paul's Scarlet rose, the soft blue-grey of *Hebe cupressoides* was smothered in pale lavender flowers, giving an almost Mediterranean effect of incense-like fragrance and cool summer pleasure. Margery felt that in June she should not concern herself too much with foliage while so many plants were giving their summer display, but the silver-grey leaves – smelling strongly of camphor – of *Chrysanthemum balsamita* made a plant worth growing. Its relative *C. balsamita balsamitoides* (costmary or alecost) has a strong smell of spearmint. Its small yellow flowers come later, on rather limp stems. The foliage of the skimmias with its glowing sheen almost more yellow than green was acceptable, as were the hibiscus which in June had a similar tinge. This seemed to become less noticeable later when they flowered, in blue, crimson or white. *Eleagnus pungens* Aurea however became deeper in tone as the season advanced. In the mixed borders, escallonias were excellent: *virgata* was a good white, but not on chalk, while Gwendolyn Anley and Apple Blossom had companionable pink flowers.

Black fennel was planted with the floribunda Rosemary rose in the border against a high wall; its purple leaves kept their colour even if the rose did not bloom, and the rose when flowering was so flat and

the early-flowering *Paeonia tenuifolia*, with its fine feathery foliage and deep red single flowers, and the single pale yellow *Paeonia mlokosewitschii* with its crimson foliage, and bright cerise seed pods in autumn.

TOWARDS JUNE

Towards June, the dicentras appeared: *Dicentra eximea*, with its white form as ground cover under shrubs and trees with the slightly taller *formosa* and its improved form Bountiful, had neither the grace nor form of *spectabilis* (bleeding heart or Dutchman's breeches). This, when set against a wall in a shady part of the garden with moisture at its feet, free from disturbance, would beautifully display its tiny hearts of pink and white swaying with every breeze.

Blue came with the forget-me-nots and the perennial *Myosotis dissitiflora* which particularly contrasted with Greenland, her greenish form of *Helleborus orientalis*. The pale green spike of *Tellima grandiflora* gave a good background to the bright pink of the early poppies and cool lavender of *Thalictrum aquilegifolium*. Visitors frequently mistook tellima for *Heuchera viridis*, but the heuchera was a darker green; and did not turn such an attractive crimson in autumn. Lily-of-the-valley would naturalise anywhere at East Lambrook, filling the air with its scent – which made her feel guilty about thinning its luxuriant growth.

Among the heathers and azaleas of the peat bed were the (doubtfully) hardy orchids *Pleione pricei* and *Pleione formosana*. Originally they had been a gamble, but eventually they established themselves well enough for *Pleione limprichtii* to be added. They did not flower as well as in an alpine house, but gave Margery the confidence to add another doubtfully hardy plant, *Arum creticum*, to the garden. This arum, with luminous deep cream flowers, is usually said to need the hottest, driest place in the garden; Margery found it flowered in damp shade under trees in a friend's garden equally successfully.

SUMMER ABUNDANCE

It was in the same garden that Margery first saw the pink and white *Lathyrus vernus*. The other forms, with vetch-like flowers of violet-blue,

and *cyaneus* in bright blue, she knew well, and eventually added the white form to her collection. They grew with the dwarf silver *Dorycnium hirsutum* with its silky leaves and pink and white flowers in a hot dry place, though the peas seemed to flower anywhere.

Another plant grown with the lathyrus was *Cheiranthus mutabilis* with flowers of purple and rose madder. The bronze and primrose wallflower Wenlock Beauty was an easy companion plant, as was the pale *Erysimum capitata. Cheiranthus* Moonlight she found difficult to place because the flowers were deeper than the name, and opened from glossy brown buds; the double yellow wallflower Harpur Crewe was also better placed alone, to flower throughout the spring. Its scented double blossoms from January to June were too good to be swamped by neighbours, and when without flowers it is a shapely plant with good foliage.

Incarvillea delavayi with large orchid-pink trumpets reminded strangers of a hardy gloxinia. It would get lost in the garden when dormant, and eventually was planted for May-flowering cover in a raised bed of snowdrops and fritillaries. In shady positions *Dentaria pinnata* in white or pale mauve-pink flowered in company with the ever-blooming *Gillenia trifoliata* with its pink and white butterfly flowers through the summer.

Trilliums needed better drainage and more time to establish than they had at East Lambrook, on a bank in the shade of willows. The first planted was the Trinity flower or wake Robin, *T. grandiflorum*, with large three-petalled white flowers 9in high; she also grew the mottled-leaved, crimson, scented *sessile*, white and pink *cernuum*, pink *stylosum* and the painted *undulatum* with claret markings on its white flowers. They were slow to settle down, but once their ground cover *Mitella breweri* with small flat leaves and green flowers was established, they regularly flowered. As May turned into June her greatest pleasure was the young leaves of *Hosta fortunei* Albopicta in pale yellow with a green edge coming through the soil. Margery's pioneering use of hostas included using them as an effective edge to a border, as the golden-variegated Madonna lily had been in the previous century.

In June, the mistakes of the planting season came to a head; she saw when she had planted too closely or had not staked efficiently. The delphiniums would in some years grow 8 to 10ft tall and become susceptible to the first gale. Margery never felt she could control them by cutting down at 12in high, as she could the Michaelmas daisies, heleniums and golden rod. Loss of her white Pacific Hybrids

at the time when the roses were at their best, could be a particular grief. She grew the double delphinium Alice Artindale with its pale porcelain-blue flowers with more success, and the low bushy Tibetan delphinium with its arching sprays of dark blue flowers. This was in pockets in the ditch garden near the bright pink *Dianthus callizonus*. Margery found that the late-flowering double polyanthus Orchid Pink usually flowered with the dark blue delphinium and planted this with the dwarf *Dicentra formosa* Bountiful with deep pink flowers and blue-grey foliage.

Difficult Plants To Place

Veratrums did not grow well at first because she did not give them sufficient water and shade. The handsome clumps with broad leaves and towering spikes of grey-green, white or dark velvety brown, were nonetheless worthwhile garden features, which remained sadly rare in other gardens.

Sticky Nelly (catchfly), *Lychnis viscaria* Splendens Plena, with its brilliant magenta rosettes, was a good plant though short-lived. She found its placing difficult, but liked it with the soft blue flax *Linum perenne* or occasionally *Campanula lactiflora* Pouffe, whose dome of soft blue against light green softened the planting. *Lychnis coronaria*, rose campion, with rose-pink flowers was similar. There was a dwarf form which did not seed itself as freely as the old form, a rich velvety red called Abbotswood Rose. Margery also grew a white one, and a greatly treasured white with a pink centre, the variety which gave this plant its popular name 'cottage maid'.

Oriental poppies flaunt their brief flash of colour during June, and a good pink grew in profusion with potentillas planted between to cover dying foliage: Potentilla Mt Etna was good for this purpose, quick-growing, with long branched silver-leaved foliage that could easily be trained upwards. Perry's White with its maroon-blotched centre was her best white poppy, and the deep pink Watermelon was attractive grown with the mauve, pink or cream *Thalictrum aquilegifolium*: even without flowers this thalictrum, with its blue-grey foliage and fluffy seed heads, looked well. *Amsonia salicifolia* was another whose quiet charm suited the poppy, with small heads of slate-blue flowers. It eventually

On the terraces summer colour was supplied by pinks and roses

made a small thicket, in contrast to the aquilegias which were always considered thin plants.

Green flowers are restful in a flowery month. *Bupleurum angulosum*, sea-green with pincushion centres, was used with the alabaster-green bells of *Galtonia princeps*, smaller than the white *G. candicans*, in a narrow bed at the bottom of a wall; the viola Haslemere in soft lavender pink gave ground cover.

A group of small woodland plants in the ditch garden flowering in June included the dwarf jack-in-the-pulpit with its greeny-brown spadix and background of three leaves. The smaller *Pinellia tuberifera* was another with a narrow green tube for a flower with a long black spadix. *Mitella breweri*, being evergreen, acted as effective ground cover. *Arisaema candidissimum* never appeared until June, and she never risked it by planting ground cover for the bare earth. Its hooded sturdy spathe, like a dazzlingly white arum 8in high, shaded with green and maroon, was followed by large handsome leaves.

JUNE ROSES AND PINKS

June means roses, and here particularly the light salmon-pink sweetly scented Albertine: she frequently said if she could grow only one rose it would be Albertine. Her next choice was the China rose, which did not have the colour or shape of Albertine.

Two favourite species roses grown were the scarlet to pinkish-yellow to crimson *Rosa mutabilis* and the green China rose Viridiflora. Once, when given a bunch of roses by a friend, she noticed that the leaves were variegated. She propagated from the cuttings three fine bushes with large loose pink flowers which still grow in the garden today and have been identified as an old German variety of the past century. Climbing Guinée rose, with strongly scented dark crimson flowers, gave good hips later if not dead-headed; so did the rugosas, such as Frau Dagmar Hastrup, whose low spreading habit made it ideal under a low wall or in a mixed border.

June was also the month of dianthus, the deep red single Brympton Red being pre-eminent for Margery. She grew it to remarkable effect in front of a clump of black fennel. The double green-eyed pink John Gray was not as distinct as the single, and tended to lie down. This fault was compensated by compact flowers with a strong scent – Margery liked it planted at nose level. The mule pinks such as Emil Paré and *multiflorus* propagated easily, and quickly made carpets of dark green foliage. Casser's Pink was so floriferous it was short-lived, and propagation was by means of sacrificing flowers. Even this was easy compared to the small crimson Napoleon III: if a nursery offered this plant and it looked strong and healthy, it was not correctly named! Margery loved the old laced pinks and at one time grew many different varieties, but most of them tended to be spindly, so that by 1960 she had reduced them to Argus, white with a maroon centre, and Pheasant's Ear, double white. The modern bright salmon-pink Doris was easier to please than the better shade of pink Day Dawn, so she placed it with *Geranium endressii*, its flowers a different pink, which made a pleasing effect.

In the rock garden the dwarf blue-grey mat of *Dianthus* Madame du Barri was covered with sweetly scented pale pink flowers: it was one of the first pinks she planted, and to complement it *Linum perenne* bloomed

all summer long. Later the doubtfully hardy *Cosmos atrosanguineus* with its scent of hot chocolate and crimson-black flowers took over, and looked as well with the flax as the dianthus had. Some of the later flowering pinks continued into July. The Holbein clove with its red single flower and the rare pink sops-in-wine lingered for a year or two. The short-lived pale yellow *Dianthus knappii* was renewed regularly for the pleasure of its moonlight-primrose flowers. The old cottage clove given her by Constance Spry continued to flower and scent the garden – she thought this the best form.

July tended to be dominated by silver plants, the best of them not reliably hardy. *Senecio leucostachys* has white fernlike foliage, and its ivory flowers made it even more valuable. Eventually it was placed against a south wall and the climbing groundsel *Senecio scandens* planted to smother it as protection. This was the type of adventurous planting which gave the garden the reputation among tidier gardeners of being a jungle. The successful overwintering of a doubtfully hardy plant was in Margery's view totally worthwhile. She kept *Artemesia arborescens*, a plant considered almost as fragile as mimosa, in the garden for many seasons by overwintering small cuttings. *Centaurea candidissima* was lifted and potted each winter. *Verbena venosa* was another almost hardy plant flowering at this time, its rich purple being used with soft pink, ivory or cherry, rather than with the rich orange tagetes of public parks; she grew it at the edge of stone paths, where the root protection usually kept it through the winter. The tall *Verbena bonariensis* with its brittle stems needed a thin iron stake to display its flowers adequately – Phyllis Reiss at Tintinhull used it in a south-wall border to excellent effect.

In the north-east corner of the front garden, near the large clump of *Helleborus corsicus*, she grew *Actaea rubra* (red baneberry); its flowers are like a small astilbe, but better are the magnificent red berries which follow them. Margery considered *Actaea alba* staggeringly beautiful with its large white berries and red stems; the first time she saw it she considered it the most prominent plant in the garden.

Iris laevigata came and went in the garden, particularly the form Rose Queen, once flowered and never forgotten. The species *laevigata* remained and grew steadily in the ditch garden, though it really needed more regular moisture. The middle of July brought more pentstemons into flower; Margery liked these for their long summer colour. The taller ones grew against the wall or among other plants for stronger support,

but some, such as the pale pink Pennington Gem, which flowered a little later, were staked. Two of her better pentstemons came from Hidcote: a medium-pink with deeper markings, Hidcote Laced, and the brilliant scarlet George Home, used in the red border there. The soft purple-blue of Sour Grapes contrasted with the soft cream of White Bedder. Crimson and scarlet were supplied by the hardier Schonholzeri in intense red, Newbury Gem, and the bright *Chelone barbata*, with the deeper glowing ruby of Garnet.

Height in the border came from a dramatic planting of Bowles' Red Rhubarb *Rheum palmatum* beside the silver and ivory flowers of *Anaphalis yedoensis* on 3ft stems, with green and silver leaves. The glaucous leaves of the lemon-yellow flowered *Thalictrum glaucum* gave added height behind.

In damp shade *Senecio smithii* soon increased, its white daisies an inch wide, with shining evergreen foliage, glistening and remaining unperturbed by the worst weather. The garden needed added flowering height in July. She used the great substance of the giant *Kniphofia northiae* with its 3ft spikes of coral to greenish-yellow to strengthen the border. Among them grew *Campanula* Burghaltii, its outsize bells in slaty-blue flowering for most of the month. In the front of the border *Polygonum emodi* with narrow bronze-red leaves and spikes of blood-red flowers glowed steadily.

At one time Margery closed the garden to visitors as July gave way to August, but by 1960 her view had changed; she took the attitude that August was the month that tested the gardener's skill. She would show how to garden for display in August without recourse to half-hardy bedding plants, relying more on mounds of foliage than in any other month. A typical planting was the cream and pale green of *Scrophularia aquatica* Variegata, with purple and golden sage, against a carpet of blue-grey othonnopsis. The borders relied upon the variegated kerria and symphoricarpos. Only rarely were annual bedding plants put in.

The light clouds of lavender flowers of *Thalictrum dipterocarpum (delavayi)* were easy companions to the dwarf pink mallow *Malva moschata*. Other mallows which associated well and liked shade were an upright form of *moschata*, and the deep pink annual *Lavatera* Loveliness – when Margery remembered to plant the seeds. The mallow will flower to Christmas, and if cut down in the spring soon makes new growth. In sunnier better-drained soil she substituted buddleias,

using the strong colour of Royal Red and the pastel blue and silver of Loch Inch. *Salvia verticillata* with its soft woolly leaves and blue-grey flowers covered the ground in front.

Herbaceous lobelias did not insist on a stream, given deep humus-rich soil. Blue *Lobelia syphilitica* was distressed during drought but bright pink Joyce and violet Jean survived better and seemed hardier, more like the tough and showy violet *Lobelia vedrariensis*. The crimson leaved *L. fulgens*, with blood-red flowers, was grown in a trough beside the garden door, facing north: the honey-coloured wall was a perfect foil. Margery preferred this plant sited where the early evening light shone through the leaves and flowers. Lobelias grown in troughs got all the water they needed, but the border ones would have grown better with damper roots. Eventually she decided to grow them with *Euphorbia pilosa* major, which flowers in early spring and by August is a mound of delicate green.

Jasminum officinale continued to flower in August, each small starry sprig heavily scenting the air. At one time she had the superior form *officinale* Major, and a gold and silver variegated form. By 1960 she had reinstated the common white form, finding no better climber for a cold north wall.

CLEMATIS FOR JULY AND AUGUST

Clematis were at their best in July. Hagley Hybrid, in shrimp and crimson fading to soft lavender, was one; *Clematis florida* Bicolor (Sieboldii) did not establish until 1956 when its white flowers with rich purple centres gave their exotic passion-flower effect to the garden. The species clematis were easier to establish and often longer-lived than the hybrids; she did much to popularise them. *Clematis macropetala* Markhamii (Markham's Pink) and the blue macropetela were not as rampant as *tangutica* with its yellow lanterns and fluffy seed heads. The pale greeny-yellow flowers, smelling of cowslips, of *rehderana* established on the east wall of the cowhouse with *Viburnum fragrans*, the single pink rose Complicata, and *C. tangutica*, a planting that produced seed heads mixed with flowers for two months on end.

Clematis orientalis, with its four waxy petals of pale green which turned through yellow to orange, started in late July and still flowered

Careful planting by the kitchen chimney ensured flowers into December

two plants growing strongly and holding each other in check.

In places where it could be controlled the small pink and white daisies of *Erigeron mucronatus* burst into their final fling of flowers. Few of the previous year's self-sown seedlings lived through a severe winter, so Margery became careful about the positions she chose for it. The deep pink schizostylis Mrs Hegarty and its later paler counterpart Viscountess Byng had the same problem, and she was surprised that the ones at the bottom of the ditch garden which made strong autumn growth were the survivors at East Lambrook.

By the end of September the *Cyclamen neapolitanum* in the hedge bordering the path leading from the Malthouse to the silver garden were showing their small pink flowers; their marbled leaves appeared after the first frosts of October. The closely allied *Cyclamen graecum* in white or pink did not flower as consistently in this position. *Liriope muscari* with its violet-purple hyacinth-like spikes grew between the grey slabs of stone in the terrace garden, where its evergreen rushy leaves made a brilliant autumn effect. Coming from China, it was not a widely known plant, but it created great comment from late September visitors. Later both a white and a variegated form were added, but all three of these

obliging and useful plants are now largely ignored by gardeners, as is the allied white-flowered *Ophiopogon spicatus*. In complete contrast to the foot-high liriopes, the enormous – sometimes 10ft – dying spikes of the biennial *Eryngium giganteum* became white and papery, earning their popular name of 'Miss Willmott's ghost': Ellen Willmott, Gertrude Jekyll's gardening contemporary, loved this plant and when she visited a garden would drop a few seeds of it when the owner was not looking.

COLOUR CONTRASTS FOR OCTOBER

More Michaelmas daisies opened each day, principally of the *amellus* type. King George in rich blue, Brilliant in deep pink and the pale pink Sonia appeared, as did the refined single Ultramarine which flowered with the reliable medium-blue Lac de Genève. *Aster ericoides* Delight, with its small white flowers on branching whippy stems, flowered with what the great gardener Mrs C.W. Earle considered the most satisfactory of all asters, *frikartii*, with lavender-blue flowers and golden centres. It starts flowering in the middle of August, and still looks well in the middle of October. It carried the grouping, if the pale pink dahlias planted with it were damaged by a late September frost.

Against the reds and golds of the leaves of autumn these blue colours made a valuable contrast, alternatives to the drifts of gentians Margery remembered at Sissinghurst on one of her return visits to Vita Sackville-West, or along the walk to the lake at Forde Abbey. Margery tried growing gentians in troughs but the restricted root run and poor drainage gave inadequate results. She tried a raised peat bed, the outside built of peat blocks; here, in a wet summer, she achieved fair success with *Gentiana* Macaulayi Newburyi and *sino-ornata*, but the seedling cultivars sent by friends, such as Inverleith and Kidbrook, did not survive. The problem was only solved by the creation of a small bed when an old stone shed was removed from the north side of the house; here greensand was laid on drainage stones, peat was added and *sino-ornata* bloomed happily in the driest summers – a good companion plant for it was the green and red flowering *Fuchsia procumbens*, which would not always overwinter. Margery liked to see white forms of all plants and grew white *Gentiana saxosa* as a fascinating alpine for its own merits. She felt the same way about the white form of

sino-ornata, but realised this was not popular among people who like their gentians blue.

Many cultivars of kniphofia or red-hot poker were considered too orange for the garden, but several in paler tones, with dwarfer habit, were grown – the ivory Maid of Orleans, the green-tipped spikes of Bees' Lemon, and the pale yellow Brimstone, with long-flowering species such as *snowdoni*, which produced bright coral spikes to the end of October, the late-flowering orange *galpinii*, and its dwarf counterpart the brighter-coloured Elf. Undergoing its hardiness trials during the early 1960s was the shaggy, showy mop-headed *Kniphofia comosa* with prominent stamens and flowers of a light clear tangerine. *Kniphofia northiae* had a position at the end of the long border, where its smooth, grey-green, stiff leaves on gigantic rosettes looked sub-tropical with its spikes of greeny-yellow flowers tipped with coral. *K. caulescens* was a small edition, its solid flowers of soft coral fading to pale greeny-yellow.

Against the variegated form of single kerria, the flaming torches of the 5ft spikes of Prince Igor gave a dramatic contrast, while the wider C.M. Pritchard with its flower heads shading from soft lemon to coral flowered in a group with a big white cottage daisy *Chrysanthemum uliginosum* and the lavender-blue *Aster frikartii*. East Lambrook was never short of flowers in October; reliance on colour and form from seed heads and foliage did not become necessary until late into November. The creamy-white plumes of cimicifugas *racemosa* and *ramosa* were at their best in the dampest areas of the garden. The intense mahogany of the tuberous *Bidens atropurpurea* of Victorian bedding, glowing with its flowers smelling of rich chocolate, was an example of the less usual plants, while *cordifolius* asters like Silver Spray, Blue Star and Elegans, with the soft blue Photograph, provided a further burst of colour.

LESS SPECTACULAR PLANTS COME FORWARD

As the growing season drew to a close, less spectacular plants had more prominence. The trailing habit, soft grey-green leaves and primrose flowers of *Antirrhinum asarina* mingled in a greensand trough

with the bright blue pea flowers of *Parochetus communis*, these two needing more care than the long-flowering golden-centred white poppy of the dawn, *Eomecon chionanthum*, which needs constant control of its suckering stems.

Origanums, now popular with the vogue for culinary herbs, were not widely grown in 1960. Finding the Bury Hill form of *Origanum vulgare*, with its heliotrope and indigo flowers in late October, was useful, as a companion for *Oxalis floribunda*. The even more attractive *Origanum laevigatum*, with its tight carpet of dark, glaucous leaves an inch off the ground, threw out small violet flowers on inch-high stems. *Serratula shawii* was another plant of considerable charm, with its small subdued mauve cornflower-like blooms nestling in ferny bronze foliage, and grown with *Geranium renardii*.

The toad lilies, tricyrtis, began to come into their own in a narrow shady bed where they could be studied quietly. *Tricyrtis hirta* had pale pink petals with purple spots, and the pure white form grew taller and more strongly; these varieties were the most satisfactory for the late October garden. *Anaphalis triplinervis* was showing its fluffy white daisies with pale gold centres: good in the garden, good as a cut flower or a dried flower, good at all times of the year, from its silver rosettes of foliage to its October flowers in mounds of white and ivory, showing up well in dark corners. It was a striking contrast to purple rhus, or for softer effect with domes of golden variegated box, golden sage or the soft grey-green of *Alchemilla mollis*. The narrow 3in leaves up the silver stems have three deep veins and are green with silver linings – the silver is emphasised as they twist and turn. Behind it towered *Thalictrum glaucum* in grey-green and soft yellow.

By late October visitors realised what an excellent plant the neat, long-flowering 9in *Aster thomsonii* was, its orange-eyed lavender-blue flowers standing out well when planted with *Sedum spectabile*. Two convolvulus in warm corners had their final blooming in late October: the delicate silver-leaved pink-and-white flowered *Convolvulus cneorum*, and *mauritanicus* with its deep blue limpet flowers, both on the margin of frost-hardiness. *Convolvulus mauritanicus* was much improved in summer by a planting of pink-flowered *Phuopsis stylosa* providing mossy-green foliage; behind it the hardy fuchsia Mrs Popple was still starred with purple and magenta.

THE BERRIES AND BRIGHT LEAVES BEGIN

Berries and leaves added vivid patches of colour to last well into the winter. The glistening white fruits of *Sorbus hupehensis* aged to a rosy sheen, the red fruits of *Sorbus vilmorinii* to a pink-blushed white. The snowberry, *Symphoricarpos* Mother of Pearl, particularly enchanted Margery: this low, spreading tree with its small clusters of long-lasting soft pink berries was only equalled by the large glistening white berries of the variety White Hedge. These two and a third snowberry, Constance Spry, grew under the shade of an apple tree near the orchard; a fourth, the deep carmine Magic Berry, did not grow or please so well.

Autumn tints and berries sometimes came together: foliage of the common spindleberry *Euonymus europaeus* turned crimson with its old-rose fruits, and in the variety *alatus* the colour became even more intense. The berries of *E. planipes (sachalinensis)* were particularly big, brilliant and attractive to birds, as were the blue berries on the bright-leaved vaccinium in the peat bed.

Stranvaesia undulata was one of East Lambrook's best shrubs for autumn. Its sideways growth filled odd corners well, it had bunches of scarlet fruit, and its scarlet and gold were long lasting. Not all the shrubs were so accommodating. *Rhus potaninii* had an attractive bark etched with grey-green and was a wonderful sight when its leaves were aflame, but a high wind, early frost or heavy rain soon finished it. The stags-horn sumach, *Rhus typhina*, with its fingered red and orange leaves and crimson fruits like candles was soon over. *Rhus typhina* Laciniata was a plant of great delicacy, making up for its faults with gentle charm.

No autumn tree was more striking than *Ginkgo biloba*, the maidenhair tree. As it turned from glaucous green to gold, it took on a new character. A slow-growing tree which did not rapidly crowd the two acres of East Lambrook, it was liked for its feeling of permanence. The scarlet oak *Quercus coccinea*, with *Hydrangea paniculata* beneath, was another of the late October sights at East Lambrook, as the great trusses of hydrangea flowers aged from white to flesh pink.

The purple vine *Vitis vinifera* Purpurea with rich claret-red foliage through the summer, in autumn produced a bloom which gave mystery to its colour. In front were the soft blue late-flowering cordifolius

asters and *Ceratostigma willmottiana*; this planting was later changed to the tender *Cobaea scandens*, to mix pale green, lilac and purple together. Planted alone as a prop for the cobaea was the brilliant autumn *Berberis thunbergii* Vermilion, with leaves and berries of bright scarlet. The smoke tree, *Cotinus coggygria* had a more subtle beauty in the distance, its bluish-green leaves turning yellow and shades of pink as the taller more brilliant *Cotinus obovatus* (formerly *Rhus cotinoides)* turned vivid orange-scarlet.

Against all this autumn colour the soft green and silver of the dwarf pampas grass *Cortaderia argentea* Pumila at the top of the steps with the grass walk behind, held the scene as the garden moved from October to November, still full of colour from leaves and stems – though condemned by some as a jungle. The knotted stems of *Physostegia* Summer Spire turned a fine shade of red, and it was eventually moved out of the narrow terrace bed to make a pleasant contrast to the silver-lined leaves of *Senecio monroii*.

As the crimson leaves of *Paeonia mlokosewitschii* and *obovata alba* turned to brown, the big leaves of the bergenias became daily brighter. *Bergenia cordifolia* with its leathery heart-shaped leaves turned crimson and *crassifolia* coloured into warm amber and red, as did a host of geranium species. The herbaceous plumbago, *Ceratostigma plumbaginoides*, with its intense, unfathomable blue flowers and crimson leaves grew steadily with the small tangerine-coloured *Potentilla tonguei*. At the base of the low walls, the leaves of the saxifrage *umbrosa geum* coloured crimson and the golden variegated form took on a brighter glow.

THE HELLEBORES AGAIN

Splashes of gold and crimson came into the dark glistening leaves of *Viburnum utile*, and one or two hellebores, such as *olympicus* began their flowering season. In some years they were joined by the rounded green flowers of *corsicus*, and always by the misnamed 'red Christmas rose', *Helleborus atrorubens*.

She tried to plant every possible cultivar of the Christmas rose *Helleborus niger*. She found among them *macranthus, altifolius*, St Brigid, St Margaret and *maximus*, but none of these was certain to flower at Christmas; the two finer, larger forms of *niger*, Eva and Potter's Wheel,

As the daffodils of spring carried the garden colour for another season, the walls of the malthouse burst into life with a fresh growth of leaves

rarely did. *Helleborus foetidus* began to show its small green buds, while the scented pale blue flowers of *Iris unguicularis* Walter Butt were almost certain to appear. Nearby the shrubby *Salvia neurepia* which had started flowering in August continued into November; it was better than any of the red varieties, a real cherry colour without a hint of blue, and leaves of light yellow-green that showed up the flowers. The sub-shrub *Salvia bethellii* is not hardy, but after blooming through the summer it was still producing its magenta flowers in November. The toughest of the salvias was *grahamii (microphylla)* which grew near the Barton gate and benefited from the bergenia in front of it, and at one time the woolly-leaved long-armed lavender-blue flowered *Salvia candelabra*. In November *Verbena venosa* was still blooming in the stones at its feet. The dainty carpeter *Pratia treadwellii* was still covering itself with small white lobelia-like flowers which finished as purple berries seeding away into the lawn, providing excellent ground cover for the golden flowers of *Sternbergia lutea*.

Gathering seed from the later-flowering plants became an added burden as the demand from the nursery increased. The nerines were good

but *Amaryllis belladonna* was not, while the latest and best of the green eryngiums, *E. pandanifolium (decaisneana)* fell between the two. It was always in demand, but its size made division impractical; the November winds snapped its heads before the seed was ripe, so there was a constant battle to get sufficient material to propagate and distribute. This applied to a whole range of late-flowering plants whose virtues she extolled in lectures. Not that all these plants were reliably hardy: many were found in Margery's gardening tours of Devon, Cornwall and Ireland, and plants like the Mexican incense bush, *Eupatorium micranthum*, with its pink-flushed-white scented gypsophila flowers would be badly hit by hard winters.

FLOWERING SHRUBS FOR NOVEMBER

The long flowering season of *Viburnum fragrans* with its pink scented flowers usually began by November and continued intermittently, as did the pink or white cherry *Prunus subhirtella* Autumnalis.

The dwarf lavender flowers of *Hebe* Primley Gem would continue in Somerset throughout the winter, though this shrub was always on the verge of frost damage. The garden usually overwintered the white and green variegated forms of *Hebe andersonii*, and the purple, crimson and lavender spikes of *speciosus* continued throughout the winter – in Margery's day these shrubs were classed as veronicas. *Clerodendrum bungei (foetidum)* would be cut to the ground every year; it was usually just about to flower when the first frosts broke, but when the clerodendrum did win the race their flat heads of rich pink flowers nestled in purple leaves. *Clerodendrum trichotomum* drowned the scent of its leaves with that of its flowers, and became a small tree with bright blue berries that never failed to attract attention.

The border of *Hydrangea hortensis* in the front garden was planted with pink and white mixed together; as her gardening developed and gaps appeared she added various species such as *H. villosa*, with its flat flowerheads of crimson, copper and green. *Hydrangea mariesii* at the north-east corner became the focal point as it spread wide-leaved, surrounded by its tiers of flat flowerheads, left to fade on the plants until spring. Around the garden *H. petiolaris* slowly faded, as did the prominently placed *H. involucrata* Hortensis which in its prime had

this garden as a low planting on beds, and against the house as a host for *Tropaeolum speciosum*. The shady corners are clothed with bergenias and hostas, *Lithospermum purpureo-caeruleum* is an under-planting for shrubs. A small garden has species hydrangeas, azaleas, heathers and coloured primroses.

Under the dry shade of a massive ilex, hardy cyclamen grow with small periwinkles and the purple-leaved *Viola labradorica*. *Geranium macrorrhizum* is another plant that does well here and the bright red single paeony *peregrina* glows under the shade of the trees. Behind a hedge a bed shaded with *Viburnum carlesii* and planted with hydrangeas has an underplanting of alpine strawberries, while on the opposite side of the path two tall liquidambers stand sentinel, and lilies-of-the-valley and *Waldsteinia ternata* do well in dry shade.

Bodnant, the National Trust Garden overlooking the Conway Valley in North Wales, is most famous for its rhododendrons. There are many other rare shrubs, including avenues of magnolias underplanted with plants like geraniums and *Helleborus corsicus*. Hellebores there are planted on the steep banks leading down to the bottom of the garden. The shady slopes are filled with smaller rhododendrons, some with glaucous foliage, and at the bottom beside the water are large-leaved rhododendrons. On the opposite bank the undergrowth is thick, but ferns grow near the water and blue hydrangeas are reflected in the river with its large moss-covered stones.

The late A.T. Johnson created a woodland garden at Bulkeley Hill near Bodnant. There are streams on each side of the garden so that there is always the gentle sound of moving water. All has passed into caring hands, the grass cut and the many interesting plants preserved. Under the magnolias, cherries and *Juniperus coxii* the ground is carpeted with plants to flower at every season. The Madeira orchid has increased to a large clump in one place, tracts of *Arisarum proboscideum* cover the ground in another, with carpets of *Omphalodes verna* and Welsh ferns. Trilliums delight in the shade and damp. *Lamium orvala* grows well on the dry banks, at one end of the garden, with *Cyclamen repandum*, epimediums, vancouverias, and *Cardamine trifolia*. Mr Johnson did not despise ordinary things and there are thick carpets of *Claytonia virginica*, and large clumps of variegated carex more commonly known as sedge. He grew all the tiarellas including the rare *Tiarella unifoliata*. In this garden the hardy fuchsia Mrs Popple is at the top of a tall shady wall, and a banksian rose on a north-east wall. The rose Canary Bird did well in the shade, and azaleas kept their colour well and lasted better.

In the gardens at Spetchley near Worcester are large trees which give

shady beds. There is an interesting formal garden in shade. The four parts of the garden are edged with stone, and in some cases the beds are on two levels. A hedge of *Euonymus radicans* Silver Queen is an interesting feature of one part of the garden. The planting included ferns, gillenias, and a smilax with whitish-green flowers. The surprise is liatris, agapanthus, pentstemon and veronicas in shade.

Beneath magnolias, yuccas grow well, *Ascelepdia warleyi* makes large plants and *Paeonia obovata willmottiae* reaches mammoth proportions. Captain Robert Berkeley is a nephew of the late Miss Willmott and grows many of her plants. Mints, bergenias, pampas grass and *Fuchsia magellanica* grow happily together with *Lonicera tragophylla*. The uncommon *Asparagus filicinus* and *Paeonia tenuifolia* grew well under a beech tree.

There is no shade in the late Lawrence Johnston's garden at Hidcote, and it can never be visited too frequently; each time a lesson is learned. Presently Mr Burrows cares for the garden for the National Trust. *Hydrangea villosa* does well in the shade, as does the large-leaved *Hydrangea sargentiana*. The ground falls away in one place under the trees, and in this part of the garden special treatment is needed for the banks. The single *Ranunculus aconitifolius* is not often seen. It is not as attractive as the double form, the fair maids of France, but when thick planting is needed it makes 2 to 3ft of fine foliage and small golden-centred white flowers. Astilbes, *Euphorbia robbiae*, hostas, gunnera and filipendula add interest; here carpeters include *Waldsteinia ternata*, small and large leaved periwinkle, and the uncommon *Vinca acutiloba*. The sweet-scented wild woodruff grows here, and the marble-leaved *Arum italicum* Marmoratum. *Alchemilla major* is planted with such geraniums as *renardii*, *macrorrhizum* and *nodosum*. *Smilacina racemosa*, *Helleborus foetidus* and pulmonarias give the garden a well-clothed look. Great clumps of *Carex monrowii* Variegata and ferns are used on the rough banks. I have always liked the way *Euphorbia wulfenii* is allowed to grow under trees, and the white-flowered *Paeonia emodi* grown naturally in shady beds. The shade in some parts of the ravine garden is dense. Here are ferns, periwinkles and the dark shining leaves of *Asarum europaeum* with the hairy leaved *Symphytum grandiflorum*. *Lithospermum doerflora* is a plant for shade. It has fleshy roots and increases well, making a foot-high forest of dark foliage for its dark purple-blue clusters of flower.

Polygonum reycoutria has room here to make a charming effect with small pink flowers and grey-green leaves. In one shady bed with a slight slope *Fragaria indica* is used to cover a wide expanse, and the combination of dark green leaves, yellow flowers and big red berries is most successful.

The University Botanical Garden at Oxford is the oldest of our botanic

gardens, and its large trees and high walls provide many shady beds. Bergenias show how well they flower in shade, *Geranium psilostemon* and many symphytums grow magnificently. It is always interesting to study the plants growing in the wall beds, white dentaria, ferns and ivies with variations of London Pride, *Saxifraga umbrosa*. Mr. G.W. Robinson the Curator is a great plantsman, one can spend days here and still find new plants to study.

Quarry Wood near Newbury has one of the most interesting collections of shrubs in the country gathered together by the late Walter Bentley. Mr and Mrs Martyn Simmons are presently devoting their energies to the preservation of the whole garden. Green paths wind among beds filled with shrubs and trees which shelter their famous collection of lilies. Epigeas need acid soil and deep shade, there are orchids, *Speirantha gardenii*, species paeonies and *Thalictrum delavayi* flowering well in shade with a good form of *Lobelia fulgens*. *Jeffersonia diphylla* and *Bergenia delavayi* grow well with podophyllum and the pink-flowered *Francoa sonchifolia*. One of the loveliest parts of the garden is an avenue of tall trees under which daffodils bloom, leaving a carpet of silvery moss for the rest of the year.

The Enfield garden of the late E.A. Bowles is typically Victorian, with large trees, pergolas and arbours. The shade did not stop Mr Bowles from growing many extraordinary plants. Anyone who has visited the garden will remember his clumps of the variegated crown imperial *Fritillaria imperialis*, growing under the trees beside the new river. The shade was ideal for his collection of snowdrops and other bulbs, many of which grow with his hellebores that included forms with both yellow and green flowers.

His mixed plantings under trees taught me a great deal. He mixed plants of different texture, colour and form to make a harmonious whole throughout the year. *Geranium ibericum* with its hairy leaves is next to the dark shining foliage of *Helleborus niger* with *Dicentra spectabilis* behind, to show off its dangling pink hearts among glaucous leaves. Amongst them grow the poisonous hemlock *Conium maculatum* with its serrated glossy leaves. He used the common ferns like crested hart's tongue and varieties of the shield fern (polystichum), with meconopsis and colchicum. The rarer ferns protected soldanellas, hepaticas and cyclamen. He grew giants and alpines under trees, *Yucca recurvifolia* and *Spiraea camtschatica* with *Gunnera chilensis* among them. Even the South American eryngiums did well in the garden which has more shade than open ground.

The shade in the garden at Sissinghurst Castle comes from walls and buildings. There are plantings of gallica roses in shade, large beds of *Gentiana sino-ornata* and the famous nut walk which used to be thickly carpeted with

polyanthus and now has other plants as well. The white and silver garden is very shady under a large tree, but this does not stop the flowering of many white-flowered plants. The tall trees are hung with *Rosa filipes* and *Clematis spooneri*. A garden like this needs formality, and white-flowered variegated geraniums are used. In the centre vase *Helichrysum petiolatum* gets very large by the end of the season, refuting the idea that all silver plants need the sun. There are santolinas, *Helichrysum trilineatum*, *Senecio leucostachys* and *Artemesia ludoviciana*, *stelleriana*, *pontica* and *absinthium*. *Anaphalis triplinervis* is a useful shade plant with silver leaves and white everlasting flowers. White physostegias and delphiniums, *Dictamnus fraxinella*, white Scotch roses and white polemoniums, violas and violets, are against a background of onopordum and *Pyrus salicifolia* behind.

Norman Hadden's small garden at West Porlock has the greatest number of rare plants in any garden in the world, much of it shaded. The ground is carpeted everywhere with cyclamen, scillas, cardamines and euphorbias. The New Zealand *Libertia brenniodes* with gold-banded grassy leaves and interesting seed heads does well in a very shady spot and everywhere are shrubs and trees from all over the world. Mutisias grow through the shrubs and camellias flower in midwinter. Almost next door is the garden made by the late Walter Butt and then developed by Mr E.B. Anderson. There are trees in the front where alliums, fritillaries and arums do well, deeper shade at the back is over helleborus, orobus and erythroniums.

Miss Nancy Lindsay has a small garden under trees at Abingdon. She is well known for her eye for a good plant, and species from all over the world are present; helleborus, paeonies, aroids, ferns and grasses to name but a few.

My advice to any owner of a shady garden is to visit as many similar ones as possible, to see what grows and what can be learnt. I am continually changing and developing my garden all the time.

Index